Generational Workplace Teams

Harness Diversity and Innovation, Problem-Solve and Propel Organizational Growth

S.B. Wade

Table of Contents

Introduction

In the bustling corridors of today's workplaces, a profound transformation is underway—one that transcends traditional boundaries and challenges long-held norms. Imagine a scenario where multiple generations, each with its unique perspectives, values, and communication styles, converge to collaborate on a shared mission. It's a tableau that reflects the changing dynamics of our modern workforce, where generational diversity has become the norm rather than the exception.

Consider this: In the United States alone, five generations—the Silent Generation, Baby Boomers, Generation X, Millennials, and Generation Z—coexist in workplaces, contributing their insights and skills to a mosaic of talents. The impact of this generational convergence is profound, shaping not only how organizations operate but also how we interact, communicate, and innovate.

Intriguingly, this generational diversity presents both opportunities and challenges. It holds the potential to infuse organizations with fresh ideas, foster creativity, and drive innovation. However, it can also give rise to misunderstandings, communication gaps, and clashes of values, if not managed effectively.

The question that emerges from this dynamic landscape is: How do we harness the collective power of generational diversity to fuel organizational success, foster a culture of inclusion, and propel our workplaces into a brighter future?

This book is your guide to answering that question.

In the following pages, we will embark on a journey through the multifaceted world of generational diversity in the workplace. We will explore the characteristics, values, and aspirations that define each generation, demystify common stereotypes, and unveil the hidden strengths that emerge when generations collaborate harmoniously. Through real-life stories, expert insights, and practical strategies, you will gain the knowledge and tools necessary to navigate this new era of work with confidence and competence.

Generational diversity is not a challenge to be overcome; it is a multitude of experiences waiting to be woven into organizational excellence. In the chapters ahead, prepare to unlock the full potential of your multigenerational workforce and embark on a journey toward a workplace that thrives on diversity, inclusion, and innovation.

Welcome to a new era of work, where generational diversity is not merely a fact but a powerful force for change.

This book equips you, the reader, with the knowledge and strategies needed to foster collaboration and harmony among multi-generational employees. In the pages that follow, we will explore generational diversity in the workplace, demystifying the differences that often lead to miscommunication and conflict.

Our mission is to transform these differences from potential challenges into powerful assets. We will present the unique characteristics, values, and expectations of each generation, allowing you to gain a profound understanding of what drives and motivates your colleagues, employees, and team members.

Through real-world stories, expert insights, and actionable advice, you will discover how to bridge generational gaps, create inclusive environments, and capitalize on the collective strengths of diverse age groups. Innovative approaches to leadership, communication, and talent management will enable your organization to thrive in a world where generational diversity is not just a reality, but a driving force of progress.

Ultimately, this book is your blueprint for fostering collaboration, unlocking innovation, and building an organizational culture where every generation can contribute their best and thrive. I hope that, armed with these insights and strategies, you will embark on a transformative journey toward a workplace that not only embraces generational diversity but thrives because of it. Together, let's shape a future where we celebrate generational differences, where generations collaborate with understanding and empathy, and where your organization becomes a beacon of excellence in the diverse landscape of the modern workplace.

In the dynamic workplace of today, where Baby Boomers, Generation X, Millennials, and Generation Z converge, the intricacies of generational diversity have never been more pronounced. As we stand at the crossroads of history, this book, *Multi-Generational Workplace Teams*, offers a compelling journey through the multi-generational landscape, decoding the generational code that shapes our professional lives. Within these pages, we will embark on a voyage to understand, embrace, and harness the power of generational diversity, while shattering the stereotypes that often divide us.

As you embark on this illuminating journey, we invite you to not only gain a deeper understanding of generational diversity but also to actively engage with the content. This book is not just an observer's guide; it's a toolkit for transformation. The insights and strategies contained within these chapters will equip you to thrive in today's diverse and ever-changing workplace.

Join us as we present generational diversity, foster unity in diversity, and create workplaces where every generation can shine. Let's begin this transformative journey together.

Chapter 1:

Decoding the Generational Code

Understanding the core characteristics, values, and work styles of each generation is the first step towards building a harmonious and productive multigenerational team.

1.1 Baby Boomers: The Loyal Veterans

In the annals of generational history, Baby Boomers stand as a significant cohort, born between 1946 and 1964. Their sturdy work ethic and unwavering loyalty to their employers often characterizes them. These traits have shaped their journey in the world of work and made them a distinct presence in today's diverse workplace.

Statistics from the Pew Research Center (Fry, 2018) reveal an intriguing facet of Baby Boomers' work lives: They have held an average of 12 jobs by the time they reached their 50s. This statistic reflects their propensity to stay committed to a single employer for extended periods, often marking entire careers within a company's walls. Such loyalty is a testament to their steadfastness and dedication. The other interesting statistic is that baby boomers are staying in the labor force at rates not seen in generations for people their age. In 2018, 53% of adults ages 54 to 72 were still working or looking for work (Fry, 2019).

One notable feature of Baby Boomers is their preference for face-to-face communication. While digital communication platforms like Slack and Zoom have become ubiquitous in modern workplaces, Baby Boomers may navigate the digital landscape with hesitation. Valuing direct, personal interaction in the workplace is a hallmark of their generation.

For Baby Boomers, job security holds a paramount place in their career aspirations. A survey conducted by Deloitte underscores this point, with a significant 66% of Baby Boomers identifying job security as a key factor in their job satisfaction (Deloitte, 2023). It is this sense of security that often motivates them, along with the prospect of holding positions of authority within their organizations.

Yet, in the evolving landscape of the workplace, Baby Boomers may sometimes face the challenges posed by younger generations who ascend the ranks with swiftness. This dynamic can create a sense of vulnerability, as the familiar terrain transforms before their eyes.

However, it's essential to recognize that Baby Boomers bring a wealth of experience and knowledge to the table. Their seasoned perspective and years of dedication make them a valuable resource in any workplace. For instance, consider Jamie Dimon, the CEO of JPMorgan Chase & Co. A Baby Boomer by birth, his leadership and extensive experience have propelled him to become one of the most esteemed figures in the banking industry, showcasing the enduring influence and contributions of this generation.

Story of Susan: Susan has been with the company for over 30 years. She values hard work, loyalty, and dedication, often spending extra hours at the office to ensure the success of her projects. Susan prefers face-to-face meetings and believes in the power of strong relationships to get work done. She often shares stories about the company's history, contributing a sense of tradition and continuity, and mentoring younger employees with the wisdom she has garnered over the years.

In the pages that follow, we will explore the generational subtleties of Baby Boomers and other cohorts, seeking to bridge the gaps and foster understanding across the multigenerational workforce. Understanding their unique attributes is the first step towards building a harmonious and productive team that leverages the strengths of each generation.

1.2 Generation X: The Independent Bridge

Their remarkable independence and self-reliance characterize generation X, spanning the birth years from 1965 to 1980. Growing up during an era marked by increasing divorce rates and a rising number of dual-working-parent households, they earned the moniker "latch-key kids." This upbringing instilled in them a sense of self-sufficiency and adaptability that continues to define their approach to life and work.

One of the defining traits of Generation X is their strong problem-solving ability. This aptitude is a product of their upbringing, where they often had to fend for themselves and find solutions to challenges without constant parental oversight. A study conducted by the Center for Generational Kinetics confirms this, shedding light on their prowess in addressing complex issues in the workplace. Gen Xers' ability to think critically and independently makes them valuable assets in problem-solving scenarios.

In seeking work-life balance, Generation X places a premium on flexibility, often prioritizing it over job security. This shift in values has prompted companies, including industry giants like Netflix, co-founded by Gen Xer Reed Hastings, to adopt flexible work policies. Such policies acknowledge the importance of accommodating diverse lifestyle needs and maintaining a healthy equilibrium between professional and personal life.

Perhaps one of the most notable roles that Generation X plays in the workplace is that of a bridge between older and younger generations. They possess the unique ability to understand and effectively communicate with both their senior colleagues and their junior counterparts. This proficiency is evident in industries like technology, where Gen X leaders such as Google's Sundar Pichai and Microsoft's Satya Nadella have successfully managed diverse, multigenerational teams.

Skeptical and Cynical: Gen Xers are often characterized as skeptical and cynical, shaped in part by events such as the Watergate scandal, economic recessions, and corporate downsizing. They question authority and are known for their pragmatism and realism.

Tech-Adaptive: While they didn't grow up with the internet as Millennials did, Gen Xers were early adopters of technology. They witnessed the transition from analog-to-digital and have adapted to technological advancements throughout their lives.

Work Ethic: Gen Xers are recognized for their strong work ethic and a commitment to their careers. They often value job security and have a tendency to stay with the same employer for longer periods compared to more recent generations.

Balancing Act: Many Gen Xers are known for their ability to balance work and family life. They came of age during a time when discussions about work-life balance gained prominence, and they often seek workplaces that offer flexibility and a healthy work-life equilibrium.

Practical and Individualistic: This generation is practical, resourceful, and individualistic. They value personal responsibility and self-reliance, attributes influenced by their upbringing as latch-key kids.

Entrepreneurship: Gen Xers have a significant presence in entrepreneurship and small business ownership. They have shown a willingness to take risks and start their own ventures, often driven by a desire for autonomy and independence.

Cultural Contributions: Gen X has made notable contributions to pop culture, including the rise of alternative music, the grunge movement, and the emergence of video games as a mainstream entertainment medium. They also witnessed the birth of the personal computer and the development of early gaming consoles.

Parenting Styles: Gen Xers have had a significant influence on modern parenting styles. As parents, they often prioritize a more hands-on approach to raising their children and may be less authoritarian than the generations that came before them.

Midlife Challenges: As Gen Xers have entered midlife, they face challenges such as caring for aging parents, planning for their own retirement, and navigating the empty nest phase as their children leave home.

Story of Michael: Michael is a middle manager who has been with the company for 15 years. Independent and resourceful, he often encourages his team to find solutions on their own. Michael balances traditional corporate communication and newer digital communication tools, often serving as a bridge between older and younger colleagues. He's seen the company evolve and values opportunities for continuous learning and development.

Generation X serves as a vital link in the generational chain, fostering collaboration and understanding between different age groups within the workforce. Their independence, problem-solving skills, and commitment to work-life balance make them adaptable and valuable contributors to today's ever-evolving professional landscape.

As we continue our journey through the generations in the workplace, we will explore the unique characteristics and contributions of each cohort, seeking to decode the generational code that shapes our modern work environment. Understanding Generation X and their role as the "Independent Bridge" is just the beginning of our exploration into the diverse and dynamic world of multigenerational teams.

1.3 Millennials: The Digital Pioneers

Millennials, the generation born between 1981 and 1996, have ushered in a new era of workplace dynamics, marked by their unparalleled comfort with technology and digital innovation. The first generation to grow up with the internet is often referred to as the "Digital Pioneers," and they have had a profound influence on the modern workforce.

Technology is an intrinsic part of Millennial DNA. They have seamlessly integrated digital tools and platforms into their lives, both personal and professional. Notably, Facebook's Mark Zuckerberg, a Millennial himself, became a household name for revolutionizing social media and digital communication, underscoring the generation's impact on the tech landscape.

One defining characteristic of Millennials is their deep-seated desire for meaningful work and a commitment to making a positive impact on the world. According to a survey conducted by Deloitte, a staggering 76% of Millennials believe that businesses should have a significant social impact (Deloitte, 2023). This emphasis on purpose-driven work distinguishes them as a generation keen on contributing to causes greater than themselves.

However, Millennials also frequently switch jobs due to their hunger for career growth and development opportunities. LinkedIn data provides insight into their job-hopping tendencies, revealing that Millennials are 50% more likely to move and 16% more likely to switch jobs than their non-Millennial counterparts are (Pandey, 2023). This proclivity to change arises from their desire to learn and progress continuously in their careers.

The intersection of technology fluency, social consciousness, and career mobility makes Millennials a dynamic force in the contemporary workplace. They bring fresh perspectives and a knack for innovation, often challenging traditional approaches and encouraging organizations to adapt to the evolving demands of the digital age.

Millennial influence extends far beyond the confines of technology, shaping the way we approach work, purpose, and societal impact in the 21st century. In the upcoming sections, we will examine their generational details and explore how they interact with other generations to drive progress and innovation in diverse workplace settings.

Several key traits and experiences characterize this generation:

Digital Pioneers: Millennials came of age during the rapid rise in the use of digital technology and the internet. They were the first generation to grow up with easy access to personal computers, the World Wide Web, and later, smartphones. This digital upbringing has shaped their communication styles, information consumption habits, and overall relationship with technology.

Millennials are often described as tech-savvy in the context of their quick adaptation to emerging technologies. They are comfortable with various digital tools, apps, and social media platforms, and they use technology for both personal and professional purposes.

Inclusive: This generation is more diverse and culturally inclusive than previous generations are. They are known for appreciating diversity, challenging traditional norms, and advocating for equality and social justice issues.

Millennials, who are highly educated, have completed college degrees or pursued advanced education in significant numbers. Millennials tend to value career development and are often characterized by their ambition and desire for professional growth.

Entrepreneurial Spirit: Many Millennials exhibit an entrepreneurial spirit, with a significant number interested in starting their own businesses or pursuing freelance and gig economy work. The rise of the startup culture and the availability of online platforms for entrepreneurship have played a role in this trend.

Financial Challenges: Millennials have faced financial challenges unique to their generation. They entered the workforce during the Great Recession (2007–2009) and have experienced issues such as high student loan debt, a competitive job market, and the challenge of homeownership in expensive housing markets.

Work-Life Balance: Millennials often prioritize work-life balance and seek workplaces that offer flexibility and meaningful work experiences. Millennials value experiences and actively seek opportunities that align with their personal values and passions.

Socially Conscious: Millennials are socially conscious and are drawn to brands and organizations that show a commitment to social and environmental responsibility. They often use their consumer choices and social media presence to support causes they believe in.

Delaying Traditional Milestones: Because of economic factors and changing priorities, many Millennials have delayed traditional life milestones such as marriage, homeownership, and starting families. They may also have a different approach to these milestones when they do decide to pursue them.

Global Perspective: Millennials are more globally connected than previous generations, thanks to the internet and social media. They have access to a wide range of global perspectives and cultures, which can influence their attitudes and beliefs.

Story of Sarah: Sarah, a marketing specialist, has been with the company for five years. She's always looking for innovative ideas, often proposing new digital marketing strategies. Sarah values work-life balance, flexible working conditions, and the opportunity to make an impact through her work. She appreciates receiving regular feedback and being involved in diverse projects that align with her values and aspirations.

Millennials are a diverse group with varying backgrounds, values, and life experiences, and they continue to play a significant role in shaping society, the workplace, and consumer trends as they progress through adulthood.

1.4 Generation Z: The Tech-Savvy Realists

Generation Z, the cohort born after 1997, represents the frontline of the digital age. Often referred to as true digital natives, they effortlessly navigate the digital landscape, showcasing their exceptional ability to multitask across multiple digital platforms with finesse.

The rise of platforms like TikTok stands as a testament to Generation Z's prowess in creating and consuming content at an unprecedented pace. Their knack for visual storytelling and engagement on platforms like TikTok exemplifies their fluency in harnessing the power of social media for communication and self-expression.

However, Generation Z is not just about digital fluency; they are also passionate advocates for social issues. This generation values diversity, equality, and authenticity, and they use their digital platforms to amplify their voices. An inspiring example of this activism is Marley Dias, a Gen Z activist who started the #1000BlackGirlBooks campaign on social media. Her mission was to promote diversity in children's literature, reflecting Gen Z's commitment to driving positive change in the world.

Influenced by growing up during the Great Recession, Generation Z has developed a realistic outlook on life. They are driven by a desire for financial stability and career security. A report published by the Pew Research Center (Parker & Igielnik, 2020) discussed that Gen Z is more focused on saving money and securing stable employment than previous generations at the same age. This pragmatic approach stems from their experiences of witnessing economic challenges and uncertainties during their formative years.

The combination of digital savviness and practicality positions Generation Z as a vital and adaptable component of the modern workforce. They bring a fresh perspective on problem-solving, innovation, and advocacy, contributing to the dynamic nature of today's workplace.

The success stories of young entrepreneurs, such as Ben Pasternak (Pasternak, 2024), who launched his first app at the tender age of 15, showcase the immense potential of Generation Z. Their ability to leverage technology, coupled with their pragmatic approach, has the power to shape industries, drive innovation, and push boundaries in ways that previous generations could only dream of.

As we explore multigenerational teams, we will further explore the unique attributes and contributions of Generation Z, the "Tech-Savvy Realists." Their influence extends beyond their digital dexterity, as they bring a strong sense of social responsibility and a pragmatic outlook that can enrich and challenge established norms in the workplace and society at large.

Here are some key characteristics and attributes associated with Generation Z:

People often refer to Gen Z as the true digital natives because they have grown up with technology and the internet from a very young age. They are highly comfortable with smartphones, social media, and digital communication tools. This digital fluency has a profound impact on their communication, entertainment, and learning preferences.

Tech-Savvy: This generation earns recognition for its tech-savviness. They are quick to adopt new apps, platforms, and devices and are often early adopters of emerging technologies. Gen Z can handle the digital landscape and use it for everything from entertainment to education.

Multitasking Skills: Gen Z is skilled at multitasking across multiple digital platforms and devices simultaneously. They can chat with friends on one screen, stream content on another, and complete schoolwork on yet another device, all while effortlessly switching between tasks.

Entrepreneurial Spirit: Many members of Gen Z exhibit entrepreneurial traits and a desire to create their own opportunities. They are more likely to consider entrepreneurship and freelancing as viable career paths, driven by the desire for independence and the ability to pursue their passions.

Social Consciousness: social issues, equality, and authenticity are very important to Gen Z. They are engaged in advocating for causes they believe in and are not afraid to express their opinions on social and political matters. Issues like climate change, racial equality, and gender diversity are often central to their concerns.

Logical and Realistic: Growing up after the Great Recession has made Gen Z focused on financial stability. They prioritize saving money and seeking stable job opportunities.

Inclusivity: Probably the most diverse generation in terms of race, ethnicity, and cultural backgrounds in the US. They embrace diversity and inclusion and are more likely to appreciate and advocate for representation and equality.

Independent Learners: With access to a vast amount of information online, its independent learning style often characterizes Gen Z. They are more likely to seek information and skills on their own, often through online courses and tutorials.

Global Perspective: Thanks to the internet and social media, Gen Z has a more global perspective than previous generations. The internet and social media expose Gen Z to a wide range of cultures, ideas, and viewpoints from around the world, which can influence their values and beliefs.

Practical and Resourceful: Gen Z is resourceful and practical for problem-solving. They are more likely to rely on online resources and DIY solutions to address challenges.

Story of Liam: Liam recently joined the company as an intern. He's a digital native, comfortable using various technologies and platforms for work. Liam looks for companies with a strong online presence and values, inclusivity, sustainability, and social responsibility. He prefers quick and efficient communication tools like instant messaging and is eager to contribute fresh ideas and learn from cross-collaboration with various teams.

Gen Z is a diverse and dynamic cohort, and a wide range of factors shapes its members, including cultural, economic, and regional influences. As Gen Z continues to enter the workforce and society, experts anticipate they will have a significant impact and influence.

1.5 Generation Alpha: A Forward Glance

The first Alpha was born in the year 2010, marking the start of Generation Alpha, which is expected to continue until around the year 2025.

Technologically Integrated: Generation Alpha is the first generation to be born entirely within the 21st century. Experts expect Generation Alpha to be the most immersed generation in technology, as they grow up with commonplace technologies such as artificial intelligence, augmented reality, and the internet.

Generation Alpha is predicted to become the most ethnically diverse and multicultural generation in the US so far because of increasing rates of immigration and intermarriage between different ethnic and cultural groups.

Climate Change Awareness: Having been born in an era where climate change is a significant global challenge, Generation Alpha will be more environmentally conscious and active in advocating for sustainable practices and policies.

Education: With the rapid advancement of technology, the education system and learning methods are also evolving. Generation Alpha is likely to experience a more personalized and technology-driven education, facilitating more efficient and tailored learning experiences.

Health: Because of advancements in medicine and an increased awareness of health and wellness, Generation Alpha can expect to live longer lives. However, they also face challenges like mental health issues, partly because of the pervasive use of technology.

Economic Landscape: Generation Alpha will enter a workforce that's drastically different from previous generations, with jobs that might not currently exist. Automation, AI, and other technological advancements will play a significant role in shaping their careers and the global economy.

Parenting: Parents of Generation Alpha, mostly millennials, adopt different parenting styles compared to previous generations, focusing more on emotional intelligence, soft skills, and fostering creativity.

Global Connectivity: Growing up in a hyper-connected world will probably make Generation Alpha more globally aware and interconnected with people from various parts of the world.

These attributes and characteristics are projections and subject to change based on global events, technological advancements, and shifts in societal values and norms.

Chapter 2:

The Power and Pitfalls of a Multigenerational Workforce

Understanding the advantages and challenges that a multigenerational workforce presents is key to fostering a productive and harmonious workplace. By leveraging the diversity in perspectives and experiences, organizations can stimulate innovation and growth. However, if not managed effectively, these differences can also lead to conflicts and misunderstandings.

2.1 Tapping into the Multigenerational Melting Pot

Workplace diversity includes not only race, sexuality, gender, or ethnicity but also generational diversity. Baby Boomers, Generation Xers, Millennials, and Generation Z compose multigenerational teams that offer a wealth of diverse experiences and perspectives. Today's workplace can leverage these diverse experiences and perspectives to drive creative problem-solving and innovation.

Consider this scenario: A Gen Z employee brings fresh, disruptive ideas to the table, driven by their innate tech-savviness and a desire for constant change. Simultaneously, a Baby Boomer, drawing upon decades of experience, provides invaluable wisdom and a steady hand to guide the execution of these innovative concepts. This interplay of perspectives exemplifies the power of a multigenerational melting pot.

Studies, such as one conducted by the Stanford Graduate School of Business, have shed light on the benefits of diverse teams (Snyder, 2004). They often outperform homogeneous ones because different generational viewpoints lead to more careful information processing and a higher propensity for innovation. This synergy can cause innovative solutions that draw from the best of each generation's strengths.

However, it's essential to recognize that these different perspectives can also be the source of disagreements and misunderstandings, if not managed effectively. A report by the Society for Human Resource Management highlights the potential for conflicts related to generational differences in impact on employee morale, productivity, and turnover rates (Gurchiek, 2020). Miscommunications stemming from distinct communication styles, work habits, or expectations can lead to frustration and tension within teams.

To unlock the full potential of a multigenerational workforce, organizations must create an environment that values and respects these differences rather than viewing them as a source of conflict. Adobe, for example, has taken proactive steps by initiating programs like AdobeForAll, aimed at fostering an inclusive workplace where every employee feels valued and heard. By promoting inclusivity, organizations can tap into the collective wisdom, creativity, and experience of their multigenerational teams, ultimately driving innovation and success. In the sections that follow, we will outline strategies for addressing the challenges and opportunities presented by this diverse team of generations in the workplace.

2.2 The Generational Divide

Communication is a cornerstone of any successful workplace, but it's also a common area where generational differences often arise. Understanding and bridging these communication gaps is crucial for fostering collaboration and avoiding misunderstandings within a multigenerational workforce.

For instance, Baby Boomers, who grew up in an era where face-to-face interactions and phone calls were the norm, often place a premium on in-person conversations. They may value the intricate and personal touch that comes with these traditional forms of communication. In contrast, Millennials and Generation Z, raised in the digital age, are more comfortable with modern digital communication platforms like Slack, Asana, or Trello. According to a survey by App Generation, over 72% of Gen Z and Millennials prefer to communicate digitally, either through text messages or social media, even in a work context. This preference underscores the evolving dynamics of workplace communication.

These differences in communication style can lead to misunderstandings, misinterpretations, and, sometimes, feelings of exclusion if not addressed proactively. To tackle the generational divide effectively, organizations must adopt a flexible communication approach that considers the preferences of all generations.

Companies like Cisco have shown success in bridging the generational communication gap. Their collaboration platform, Webex Teams, offers a versatile range of communication options. This includes video conferencing for those who prefer face-to-face interactions, instant messaging for quick and informal exchanges, and traditional email for those who value more structured written communication. By providing a spectrum of communication tools, organizations like Cisco ensure that team members from all generations can engage in ways that suit their comfort levels and work styles.

It is essential to promote mutual understanding and empathy across generations regarding their communication preferences. Encouraging open dialogue and emphasizing the value that each generation brings to the table can help reduce potential friction. Providing training and resources to help employees adapt to new communication technologies can facilitate smoother interactions within multigenerational teams.

As we continue our exploration of the multigenerational workforce, we will examine strategies for enhancing communication, collaboration, and harmony among employees of all ages. Effective communication is not only a key to bridging generational divides but also a foundation for driving innovation and productivity in today's diverse and dynamic workplace.

2.3 Fostering Cross-Generational Collaboration

In a diverse multigenerational workforce, fostering cross-generational collaboration is not only beneficial, but also essential for promoting understanding and mutual respect among team members. Collaborative tasks and projects can serve as effective bridges across generational divides.

One notable approach to enhancing cross-generational collaboration is the concept of reverse mentoring. In this arrangement, younger employees take on the role of mentors, sharing their knowledge and expertise, particularly in areas such as technology, with their older counterparts. This practice not only facilitates cross-generational learning, but also helps break down stereotypes and preconceived notions. Jack Welch, the former CEO of General Electric, popularized this concept and recognized its potential to harness the digital skills of younger employees to benefit the entire organization (Jordan & Sorell, 2019).

However, cross-generational collaboration is not solely about technology transfer. It also entails acknowledging and respecting the diverse work-life balance expectations of each generation. For instance, Baby Boomers, who grew up in a different era, often exhibit a strong work ethic and will put in long hours. Younger generations, like Millennials and Gen Z prioritize a healthy work-life balance and seek flexibility in their work arrangements.

To create a harmonious work environment that accommodates these differing expectations, organizations need to be flexible and adaptive. They must recognize that one size does not fit all when it comes to work-life balance. Some employees may thrive on traditional work schedules, while others may excel in more flexible arrangements.

Companies like Salesforce have successfully implemented flexible work policies that cater to the diverse work-life balance needs of their multigenerational workforce. These policies allow employees to choose the work arrangements that best suit their lifestyles and responsibilities. By providing such flexibility, organizations not only attract and retain talent across generations but also create an inclusive and understanding workplace culture.

Effective cross-generational collaboration goes beyond age-related stereotypes and biases. Creating an inclusive work environment where each generation's strengths and perspectives are valued and leveraged for the benefit of the organization requires a genuine commitment. In the sections that follow, we will explore additional strategies for building trust, adaptive leadership, and dispelling biases and stereotypes within multigenerational teams.

2.4 Leading a Multigenerational Workforce

In this dynamic work environment, leading a multigenerational team has become an increasingly common challenge for managers and leaders across various industries. With teams comprising Baby Boomers, Gen X, Millennials, and Gen Z, each bringing their unique perspectives, work ethics, and communication styles, adaptive leadership skills are more critical than ever. This section delves into the strategies and practices for effectively leading a multigenerational workforce, ensuring that the diverse needs and expectations of each generation are met while fostering a cohesive and productive team environment.

Understanding Generational Differences

The first step in leading a multigenerational workforce is to understand the characteristics, values, and work preferences of each generation. Baby Boomers, for instance, value stability and are known for their strong work ethic. Gen X employees value independence and tend to be self-sufficient. Millennials prioritize work-life balance and seek purpose in their work. The youngest of the workforce, Gen Z, values innovation, seeks feedback, and desires hands-on guidance as they navigate the beginning of their careers.

Adaptive Leadership Style

Adaptive leadership is pivotal in managing a multigenerational team effectively. This approach involves recognizing and adapting to the diverse needs of team members. For instance, a Gen Z employee may benefit from more hands-on guidance and regular feedback as they enter the workforce. In contrast, a Gen X employee, known for their independence, might excel with a more hands-off approach, appreciating autonomy over their projects. Leaders who successfully adapt their style based on their team's varied needs and preferences often achieve better outcomes. This adaptability can manifest in different ways, from personalized communication methods to tailored motivational strategies.

Implementing Tailored Communication

Communication is key in a multigenerational workforce. The preferred communication channels may vary widely, from traditional emails favored by older generations to instant messaging apps preferred by younger employees. Leaders should strive to accommodate these preferences by employing a range of communication tools and techniques. This flexibility not only ensures effective communication across the team but also demonstrates a respect for individual preferences, fostering a more inclusive and engaged team culture.

Fostering Inclusivity and Collaboration

Creating an environment that celebrates diversity and encourages collaboration among different generations is crucial. Leaders should highlight the unique strengths and perspectives each generation brings to the table, leveraging these differences to foster innovation and creativity. Activities that promote cross-generational mentorship and teamwork can also help in breaking down stereotypes and building mutual respect among team members.

Continuous Learning and Development

Finally, a focus on continuous learning and development can unite a multigenerational team with a common goal of growth. Providing opportunities for professional development, whether through training, workshops, or mentorship programs, can cater to the career aspirations and learning preferences of all team members. This not only aids in skill development but also in building a culture of lifelong learning and adaptability.

Navigating Bias and Favoritism in Multigenerational Teams

A significant challenge in leading multigenerational teams is the inherent risk of bias and favoritism, which can undermine team cohesion and productivity. An Earnst and Young survey (Earnst & Young, 2023) revealed that a vast majority of employees perceive a considerable amount of bias in how individuals of different ages are treated within the workplace. This perception can lead to divisions within the team, affecting morale and, ultimately, the quality of work produced.

Recognizing and Addressing Bias

Leaders must first acknowledge the existence of generational biases and the forms they can take, from preferential treatment based on age to misconceptions about an individual's capability or work ethic. Recognizing these biases requires a level of self-awareness and a commitment to fairness and equality. Leaders should actively seek feedback from their teams about how these dynamics play out and be vigilant in their self-reflection and interactions with team members.

Implementing regular training on diversity, equity, and inclusion can help raise awareness among leaders and team members about the nuances of age-related bias and its impact. Encouraging open discussions about ageism and other forms of bias in the workplace can also foster a culture of transparency and mutual respect.

Promoting Fairness and Equity

To counteract the tendency toward favoritism, leaders should establish clear, objective criteria for evaluating performance, setting goals, and providing opportunities for advancement. This approach ensures that all team members, regardless of their generational cohort, are assessed based on their contributions and achievements rather than their age.

Regular check-ins and performance reviews can offer a structured opportunity for feedback and discussion, ensuring that all employees feel heard and valued. Additionally, creating a diverse leadership team can provide varied perspectives and help in identifying and addressing unconscious biases.

Accenture's Approach to Multigenerational Leadership Development

Accenture has emerged as a leader in addressing the challenges of leading multigenerational teams by implementing its Future Leaders Program. This initiative represents a forward-thinking approach to leadership development, specifically tailored to embrace the diversity of today's workforce.

Future Leaders Program: A Model for Success

Accenture's Future Leaders Program (Accenture, 2024) is designed to equip leaders with the skills and knowledge necessary to manage the complexities of a diverse team effectively. It emphasizes understanding the unique dynamics of multigenerational teams and fosters an inclusive culture that values each individual's contributions.

Key components of the program include workshops on managing diverse teams, strategies for inclusive leadership, and tools for mitigating unconscious bias. By focusing on these areas, the program helps leaders to not only recognize their own biases but also to develop strategies for building a more cohesive and productive team environment.

Fostering an Inclusive Culture

One of the primary goals of the Future Leaders Program is to promote an inclusive culture within the organization. This involves training leaders to appreciate and leverage the diverse perspectives and experiences of their team members, thereby enhancing innovation and creativity.

The program also encourages leaders to create opportunities for cross-generational mentorship and collaboration, which can help break down barriers and foster a sense of unity and respect among team members. By prioritizing inclusivity and collaboration, Accenture demonstrates a commitment to harnessing the full potential of its diverse workforce (Accenture, 2024).

2.5 Embracing the Future: A Multigenerational Workforce

Organizations that wholeheartedly embrace the diversity of a multigenerational workforce gain a significant competitive edge. Rather than viewing generational diversity as a challenge, forward-thinking companies recognize it as a powerful opportunity for growth, innovation, and long-term success.

Research, such as the study conducted by Deloitte, underscores the profound impact of an inclusive culture within organizations (Bourke & Dillon, 2018). Companies that cultivate inclusive environments are not only twice as likely to meet or exceed financial targets but also three times as likely to be high-performing. They are six times more likely to be innovative and agile, responding effectively to the ever-changing demands of the market.

Embracing the multigenerational workforce means leveraging the collective wisdom, skills, and experiences of Baby Boomers, Generation Xers, Millennials, and Generation Z. Each generation brings unique insights and perspectives to the table, enriching problem-solving, creativity, and decision-making processes.

Companies like Unilever have recognized the transformative potential of diversity and inclusion, integrating these principles into their core business strategies. For such organizations, diversity is not merely a checkbox, but a driving force behind innovation and business performance. Unilever, under the leadership of Paul Polman, former CEO, has made significant strides in creating a workplace where diversity is celebrated and nurtured (Poleman, 2013).

Paul Polman aptly noted, "We need to recognize that diversity is a source of innovation, it's a source of better decision-making, it's a source of more satisfaction for people." This perspective aligns with the experiences of companies that have successfully embraced generational diversity and thrived.

By embracing the multigenerational workforce, organizations can create a workplace that is more inclusive, innovative, and competitive—a workplace that is well-prepared to meet the challenges and opportunities of the future. As we move forward in our exploration of multigenerational dynamics in the workplace, we will outline practical strategies for promoting unity in diversity, dispelling biases, and fostering collaboration among employees of all ages.

Harnessing the power of a multigenerational workforce involves a strategic combination of team activities and personal leadership strategies. Activities should promote mutual understanding, reduce biases, and foster a collaborative environment, while personal strategies should focus on adaptability, continuous improvement, and the promotion of an inclusive and positive team culture.

Group Activities

1. Panel Discussion on Generational Perspectives

   Objective: Share and learn about the different generational experiences and viewpoints in the workplace.

   Activity: Organize a panel where representatives from each generation share their work experiences, motivations, and challenges.

   Outcome: Enhances mutual understanding and appreciation of diversity in the team.

2. Knowledge Sharing Sessions

   Objective: Leverage the diverse knowledge and experiences within the team.

   Activity: Conduct sessions where team members can share expertise, industry insights, or skills, promoting cross-generational learning.

   Outcome: Facilitates learning, collaboration, and knowledge transfer across generations.

3. Workstyle Workshops

   Objective: Explore various work styles present in the multigenerational workforce.

   Activity: Workshops where teams discuss their preferred work styles, communication preferences, and explore ways to work effectively together.

   Outcome: Promotes understanding and adaptation to different work styles.

4. Generational Stereotype Debunking

   Objective: Reduce biases and stereotypes related to different generations.

   Activity: Engage in discussions or activities that challenge common generational stereotypes and promote a more detailed understanding.

   Outcome: Encourages openness and reduces the impact of generational biases.

Personal Strategies for Managers

1. Flexible Leadership Styles

    Adapt your leadership style to cater to the diverse needs and preferences of your team. Different generations may respond better to varied leadership approaches.

2. Continuous Learning

    Stay informed about the latest trends, challenges, and best practices related to managing multigenerational teams. Continuous learning will enhance your effectiveness as a leader.

3. Promote Inclusivity

    Ensure that all team members are included, and their voices and opinions are valued.

4. Customize Communication

    Tailor your communication style to resonate with different team members. Consider generational preferences in communication tools and techniques.

5. Mentoring and Coaching

    Mentor and coach team members, facilitating their professional development. Consider setting up mentoring relationships within the team as well.

6. Foster a Positive Culture

    Cultivate a team culture that values diversity, collaboration, and mutual respect. Promote behaviors that contribute to a positive team environment.

Chapter 3

Tuning Into Generational Frequencies: Mastering the Art of Communication Across Ages

Understanding and adapting to the unique communication preferences of each generation can significantly enhance team dynamics and productivity. This chapter will provide readers with practical strategies to facilitate effective communication across generations, helping them bridge gaps and foster a more inclusive and collaborative workspace.

3.1 Decoding the Generations

Effective communication is the cornerstone of any successful team, and in a multigenerational workplace, it's essential to recognize and adapt to the distinct lingos and communication styles of each generation. The cultural and technological landscape of their formative years heavily influences each generation's communication preferences.

Baby Boomers, born between 1946 and 1964

Comfort and Familiarity: Baby Boomers stick with what they know. They grew up in an era where communication was more traditional, such as face-to-face, phone calls, and later, emails.

Value of Relationship Building: They often value interpersonal connections and building relationships through more personal communication methods, such as in-person meetings.

Baby Boomers are often more comfortable with formal and face-to-face communication. They value directness, clarity, and a personal touch in their interactions. Research, such as a study from the University of Arizona in 2018 (Swanson et al, 2018) highlights their preference for straightforward and structured communication. Understanding their inclination towards in-person or phone conversations can help build rapport and trust.

Baby Boomer Communication Preferences:

- Email: A standard form of communication in the professional setting, widely used and accepted by Baby Boomers.

- Landline Phones: Comfortable with traditional phone calls for direct communication.

- In-Person Meetings: Prefer face-to-face meetings to build relationships and discuss matters thoroughly.

Generation X, born between 1965 and 1980

Adaptability: Gen Xers came of age during a period of technological evolution. They adapted from initial traditional forms of communication to embracing emails and early internet technologies.

Balance: They often find a balance between the old and the new, being comfortable with a variety of communication tools, thus displaying flexibility in adapting to the recipient's preferences.

Generation X came of age during the rise of email and witnessed the emergence of digital communication. They appreciate a balanced mix of digital and personal interaction. A report from the 15th International Conference on Cognition and Exploratory learning in the Digital Age in 2018 suggests that Gen Xers value clear and concise communication without unnecessary fluff (Swanson et al, 2018). Providing them with well-structured messages can enhance their engagement and understanding.

Gen X Communication Preferences:

- Email: Frequently used for formal communication, project updates, and sharing information.

- Mobile Phones (Calls and SMS): Open to using text messages and mobile calls for quicker, more direct conversations.

- Video Conferencing (e.g., Zoom, Skype): Familiar with virtual meetings for team discussions and client interactions.

Millennials, born between 1981 and 1996

The Digital Natives, who grew up during the advent of the internet and fast-paced technological advancements, are accustomed to instant access to information and communication.

Efficiency and Convenience: Their preference is for communication tools that offer quick and real-time responses, such as instant messaging and social media. They often seek platforms that support multitasking and efficiency.

The nickname "texting generation" is often given to Millennials. Transparency and inclusivity in conversations are crucial to them. Forbes, in a 2019 article (Velumyan, 2019), highlighted their preference for straightforward and collaborative communication. Engaging with them through digital platforms and being open to feedback can facilitate effective communication.

Millennial Communication Preferences:

- Instant Messaging and Chat Apps (e.g., Slack, Microsoft Teams): Used for quick queries, team collaboration, and informal conversations.

- Social Media (LinkedIn, Twitter): Used for professional networking, staying updated with industry trends, and sharing thought leadership.

- Collaboration Tools (e.g., Google Workspace, Trello): Employed for project management, document sharing, and collaborative editing.

Generation Z, born after 1997

Because of their exposure to advanced technology from a young age, they willingly explore various modern communication platforms, including augmented reality, interactive platforms, and more.

Visual and Interactive: There is a preference for communication that is visual, interactive, and engaging. This generation often gravitates toward platforms that allow for creativity and expression, such as Instagram, TikTok, and Snapchat.

Generation Z are true digital natives. They are comfortable with instant messaging, social media platforms, and prefer visual, interactive, and bite-sized communication. Research by Swanson et al, 2018 shows Gen Zs inclination towards digital and visually engaging content. Using visual aids, interactive tools, and concise messages can enhance communication with Gen Z members.

Gen Z Communication Preferences:

- Social Media (Instagram, Snapchat, TikTok): Actively used for personal branding, networking, and staying informed about industry innovations.

- Augmented Reality (AR) and Virtual Reality (VR) Platforms: Open to exploring new technologies for immersive learning and communication.

- Interactive Platforms (e.g., Discord, Clubhouse): Engage in communities for discussions, networking, and collaborative learning.

Universal Psychological Aspects Across Generations

Regardless of their generation, people choose communication tools based on their ability to foster connection, whether through traditional face-to-face interactions or modern social media platforms.

Ease and Accessibility: Tools and platforms that are user-friendly, easily accessible, and facilitate smooth communication are preferred across generations.

Purpose and Context: The purpose of communication often drives the choice of tools. Professional, formal communication might lean toward email, while quick, informal communication may use instant messaging or social media.

Universal Tools Across Generations:

- Email: Remains a universal tool for formal communication across all generations.

- Video Conferencing Tools (Zoom, Microsoft Teams): Widely adopted across generations, especially because of the increase in remote work.

Understanding the generations is the first step towards bridging communication gaps and fostering a more inclusive and collaborative workspace. In the sections that follow, we will examine practical strategies for tailoring communication approaches to each generation, enabling effective cross-generational interactions and ultimately contributing to a harmonious and productive work environment.

3.2 Bridging the Communication Gap

In the multigenerational workplace, harmonizing communication styles involves not only understanding but also accommodating these diverse preferences to ensure a smooth flow of information and productive collaboration among team members. Recognizing and addressing the generational communication gap is key to fostering a cohesive and high-performing workforce.

One effective approach to bridging this gap is to blend communication methods during team meetings. For example, combining in-person discussions with digital tools can cater to the preferences of both Baby Boomers and Generation Z. Companies like IBM, as early as 2018, successfully implemented such hybrid communication methods (Sharma, 2019). This approach allows Baby Boomers to engage in face-to-face discussions, which they often prefer for its personal touch, while also accommodating Gen Z's comfort with digital platforms. Striking this balance can ensure that all team members feel valued and included in communication processes.

Encouraging open conversations about communication preferences can also be highly beneficial. A Gallup report from 2020 suggests that such discussions can help in setting clear expectations and minimizing misunderstandings (Brown & Robison, 2020). By creating a culture where team members feel comfortable discussing their preferred communication methods and receiving feedback, organizations can proactively address potential conflicts and create an environment that promotes understanding and flexibility.

We can organize training sessions to familiarize older generations with digital communication platforms. This proactive approach, as exemplified by Walmart in 2020, ensures inclusivity and ease of communication across all generations (Walmart, 2021). Providing training and resources to bridge the digital divide not only enhances intergenerational communication but also empowers older team members to adapt to evolving workplace technologies, contributing to their professional growth and development.

By implementing these strategies and encouraging adaptability among team members, organizations can bridge the generational communication gap effectively. As a result, communication flows smoothly, misunderstandings are minimized, and collaboration thrives, ultimately contributing to enhanced productivity and a more harmonious work environment.

3.3 Embracing Technological Tools for Effective Communication

Embracing technology plays a pivotal role in bridging the communication gap within a multigenerational team. Leveraging the right tools and platforms can help create an inclusive communication environment that accommodates the diverse preferences of each generation.

Platforms like Microsoft Teams and Google Workspace, as recommended by a Gartner report in 2019, offer versatile solutions for communication within multigenerational teams (Gartner Research, 2019). These platforms provide a balanced mix of formal and informal communication channels, catering to the needs of different generations. While Baby Boomers may appreciate the formality of email and structured documents, younger generations, like Millennials and Gen Z may prefer the ease of instant messaging and collaborative document editing. These platforms enable teams to transition seamlessly between various communication modes, ensuring that everyone can engage in a way that suits their comfort level.

Innovative companies like Procter & Gamble, as early as 2018, have introduced reverse mentoring programs to facilitate intergenerational learning and bridge the digital divide (ABDO, 2018). In these programs, younger employees take on the role of mentors, helping their older colleagues navigate through digital tools and technologies. This approach not only enhances the digital literacy of older team members, but also fosters a sense of collaboration and mutual respect among generations.

Regular feedback sessions, as practiced by Intel in 2020, are another effective strategy for identifying and addressing communication challenges promptly (Hirsch, 2020).

Encouraging open and ongoing discussions about communication processes allows teams to adapt and refine their methods based on real-time feedback. This proactive approach can help minimize misunderstandings and improve communication effectiveness across generations.

Staying informed about emerging communication technologies and trends is essential for organizations looking to bridge the generational communication gap. New tools and platforms continuously enter the market, and being aware of these developments allows companies to stay agile and adapt their communication strategies accordingly.

Incorporating technology effectively into communication processes not only enhances productivity but also shows an organization's commitment to creating an inclusive and adaptable workplace. By embracing technological tools and fostering intergenerational learning, organizations can foster a culture of continuous improvement and ensure that communication remains a catalyst for success in a multigenerational workforce.

3.4 The Role of Empathy in Cross-Generational Communication

Empathy serves as a fundamental cornerstone in bridging the generational communication gap within a diverse workplace. It's not merely about understanding different communication styles, but also about actively acknowledging and respecting them. By cultivating empathy, organizations can create a more harmonious, productive, and inclusive work environment where all generations feel valued and heard.

One key strategy in fostering empathy is encouraging active listening. Active listening involves not only hearing but also comprehending and respecting others' perspectives. This skill can be especially useful in multigenerational teams, where diverse viewpoints often emerge. By actively engaging with what others are saying and attempting to understand their unique communication styles and preferences, team members can build rapport and mutual respect.

Regular team-building activities, like those conducted by companies like Google in 2019, can also play a vital role in building empathy and understanding among team members of different generations (Burnison, 2019). These activities provide opportunities for team members to interact in a relaxed, non-work setting, facilitating the development of personal connections and a deeper understanding of each other's perspectives. By engaging in such activities, team members can break down generational stereotypes and biases, fostering a culture of collaboration and empathy.

Promoting a culture of respect and openness is essential for effective cross-generational communication. This culture ensures that each generation feels comfortable expressing themselves and contributing their unique insights. By encouraging constructive feedback and creating an atmosphere where opinions are valued, regardless of age, everyone is encouraged to communicate more effectively.

Empathy also extends to recognizing and accommodating the diverse life experiences and needs of team members across generations. For example, understanding that Baby Boomers may have different caregiving responsibilities than Millennials or that Gen Z may have unique financial concerns can foster empathy and inform supportive workplace policies.

Ultimately, empathy serves as the glue that holds together effective cross-generational communication. When organizations prioritize empathy in their workplace culture, they create an environment where team members not only understand one another's communication styles but also respect and value them. This leads to improved collaboration, reduced conflicts, and a more harmonious work environment for all generations.

Effective communication is crucial in multi-generational teams to foster understanding, reduce misconceptions, and enhance collaboration. The following exercises facilitate better communication among multi-generational team members by promoting understanding, respect, and open dialogue. They can help in minimizing misunderstandings, fostering a collaborative atmosphere, and leveraging the diverse strengths of a multi-generational workforce. Remember to tailor these activities to meet the specific needs and dynamics of your team.

Group Activities

1. Role Reversal Exercise

    Objective: Encourage empathy and an understanding of different generational perspectives.

    Exercise: Pair up team members from different generations and have them swap roles for a day or a few hours.

    Outcome: This helps team members appreciate the challenges and perspectives of their colleagues, fostering mutual respect and understanding.

2. Communication Style Workshop

    Objective: Understand different communication preferences.

Exercise: Conduct a workshop discussing various communication styles, emphasizing the differences and similarities among generations.

Outcome: Team members will be more considerate and adaptable in their communication approaches, respecting each generation's preferences.

3. Roundtable Discussions

Objective: Promote open communication and sharing of ideas.

Exercise: Organize sessions where team members can discuss projects, industry trends, or any other relevant topics in an informal setting.

Outcome: Facilitates open dialogue, idea sharing, and enhances team cohesion.

4. Scenario-Based Problem Solving

Objective: Enhance team collaboration and decision-making.

Exercise: Present the team with work-related scenarios or challenges, encouraging them to communicate and collaborate to find solutions.

Outcome: Helps in developing problem-solving skills and promotes effective communication strategies.

5. Reverse Mentoring

Objective: Leverage the diverse skill sets within the team.

Exercise: Pair younger team members with more experienced ones, allowing knowledge and skill exchange in areas such as technology, industry insights, and different approaches to work.

Outcome: Fosters mutual learning, respect, and improves communication between different generations.

6. Feedback Sessions

    Objective: Promote a culture of continuous improvement and openness.

    Exercise: Schedule regular feedback sessions, allowing team members to express their thoughts, ideas, and areas for improvement.

    Outcome: Creates a supportive environment where team members feel valued and heard.

7. "Walk in Their Shoes" Activity

    Objective: Foster empathy and understanding.

    Exercise: Have team members share their typical workday experiences and challenges, encouraging others to listen actively and ask questions.

    Outcome: Enhances appreciation of different roles within the team and improves interpersonal communication.

8. Team Debates

    Objective: Encourage critical thinking and articulate communication.

    Exercise: Organize debates where team members can discuss various work-related topics, ensuring participation from all generations.

    Outcome: Helps in honing communication skills and promotes a culture of healthy discussion and diversity of thought.

Chapter 4:

Building Trust Across Generations: The Backbone of Synergy

Trust, a non-negotiable factor for any successful team, can be challenging in a multi-generational workplace due to preconceived notions and biases. This chapter will offer real-life examples and practical advice on how to foster trust across generations, emphasizing the importance of mutual respect and open communication.

4.1 Understanding the Role of Trust in a Multi-generational Workplace

Trust is fundamental in a multi-generational workplace. Successful team dynamics are built upon the foundation of trust. Trust is important for improving communication, collaboration, and overall job satisfaction among team members of various ages and experiences.

Building Trust

To build trust, promote open communication. Encourage team members to share their ideas and opinions. This creates a sense of belonging and value among team members, which is essential for trust.

Bridging Generational Gaps

Trust helps in bridging generational gaps. When there's trust, people feel more comfortable sharing their views and experiences. This helps in reducing misunderstandings and biases that may exist because of generational differences.

Reducing Stereotypes

Trust helps in looking beyond stereotypes. When team members trust each other, they are less likely to judge based on age or generational characteristics. Instead, they focus on individual skills and contributions.

Enhancing Collaboration

Trust enhances collaboration. In a trusting environment, team members are more willing to work together, share responsibilities, and collaborate on projects, regardless of generational differences.

Facilitating Job Satisfaction

Trust improves job satisfaction. Employees feel happier and more satisfied when they know they can trust their colleagues. This improves the overall work environment and productivity.

Encouraging Engagement

Trust encourages engagement. Employees who trust their team members feel more connected to their jobs and are more likely to be engaged and committed to their work and their organization.

Trust plays a significant role in managing and improving the dynamics of a multi-generational team. Promoting trust should be a priority for organizations aiming to leverage the diverse strengths of a multi-generational workforce. By fostering trust, organizations can create a more inclusive, collaborative, and effective team, ready to meet the challenges of a modern workplace.

4.2 Strategies for Building Trust Across Generations

Building trust across multiple generations in a workplace makes for a harmonious and productive environment. Various strategies can cultivate this trust, enhancing team synergy and mutual respect among team members.

Open Communication

Transparent communication stands as a cornerstone of building trust across generations. For instance, Johnson & Johnson promoted trust among its employees through a commitment to open communication, from the top leadership down to the general staff (Waldstreicher, 2021). This strategy ensures that every employee, irrespective of their generation, feels valued and trusted.

A research report by the University of Oxford in 2012 also emphasized the significance of open communication channels in a multigenerational workforce (Green et al, 2012). Such openness can clear misunderstandings, promote inclusivity, and facilitate a cohesive working environment.

Collaboration and Team-Building Activities

Encouraging activities that promote team collaboration is another effective strategy. For example, a 2016 McKinsey report cited how Amazon employs cross-generational team-building activities to enhance trust and collaboration among its workforce (Schaubroeck et al., 2016). Such activities enable team members to understand each other beyond generational labels, promoting stronger interpersonal relationships. Team-building exercises foster understanding and empathy, improving trust among different generational members.

Constructive Feedback and Recognition

Providing employees with constructive feedback and recognizing their contributions is also instrumental in trust-building. According to a 2018 University of Pennsylvania study, feedback and recognition make employees feel valued, an essential aspect of cultivating trust (O'Flaherty, 2021).

Companies such as Salesforce have embraced regular feedback mechanisms, allowing employees of all generations to express their thoughts and ideas. This inclusivity fosters an environment of mutual respect and trust among the workforce, irrespective of their generational identities.

Adopting strategies such as promoting open communication, encouraging collaborative activities, and providing constructive feedback and recognition, are pivotal in building trust in a multigenerational workforce. These approaches contribute to creating a respectful, understanding, and cohesive team environment.

4.3 Overcoming Generational Trust Barriers

In a multi-generational workplace, overcoming trust barriers is essential for fostering a harmonious and productive environment. Different strategies, such as addressing biases and encouraging mutual respect, can help to navigate these challenges.

Addressing Biases and Stereotypes

A crucial step in enhancing trust across generations is addressing and dismantling biases and stereotypes. For instance, IBM's 2020 report highlights the company's strategy of organizing diversity and inclusion training to confront generational biases (IBM, 2020). Such initiatives help break down preconceived notions and stereotypes, paving the way for improved trust and collaboration among employees of various age groups.

The significance of recognizing and addressing biases bolsters trust levels within multi-generational teams. Understanding the roots of these biases and actively working towards eliminating them is fundamental for cultivating a trustworthy team environment.

Promoting Mutual Respect and Understanding

Fostering a workplace culture that values mutual respect and understanding is also vital. Companies like Toyota, as cited in a 2018 Deloitte report, have successfully cultivated a culture where respect and understanding flourish, enhancing trust among multi-generational team members (Deloitte, 2018). A culture emphasizing respect and mutual understanding can help overcome trust barriers that may arise because of generational differences. Such an environment enables individuals to appreciate the diverse strengths and perspectives that each generation brings, facilitating better collaboration and team cohesion.

Resolving generational trust barriers involves a strategic effort to minimize biases and promote a culture of respect and understanding. By implementing initiatives that address stereotypes and foster a respectful and inclusive environment, organizations can significantly improve trust among team members, regardless of their generational affiliations. This approach leads to a more cohesive, collaborative, and effective multi-generational team.

4.4 Nurturing Trust: A Continuous Process

Establishing trust, a fundamental component of effective team dynamics, does not happen overnight. Instead, sustained effort and dedication from team members nurtures trust continuously, ensuring that the multi-generational workforce remains cohesive and productive.

Continuous Investment in Trust-Building

Organizations benefit significantly from making trust-building a continuous aspect of their organizational culture. A notable example is Google which continuously invests in trust-building initiatives. These initiatives contribute immensely to fostering a productive multi-generational team. Such persistent efforts symbolize a commitment to nurturing a trusting and collaborative work environment. Trust-building should be an ongoing endeavor. It necessitates regular and deliberate efforts to maintain and enhance trust within teams, ensuring sustainability and improvement in team relations.

Mechanisms for Continuous Nurturing of Trust

Employing mechanisms, such as regular check-ins, feedback sessions, and open forums, also play a pivotal role in nurturing trust. Microsoft provides a robust example of this strategy in action. Under CEO Satya Nadella's leadership, Microsoft conducts consistent check-ins and feedback sessions, promoting continuous dialogue among team members across generations.

These practices facilitate timely addressing of trust issues, ensuring the maintenance of a healthy team environment. Team members regularly communicate to foster an atmosphere where issues are promptly addressed and resolved. This practice ensures the maintenance of a healthy team environment and prevents the accumulation of unresolved concerns, thus keeping trust intact.

Nurturing trust is a relentless process that demands constant attention and action. Through continuous investments in trust-building initiatives, regular maintenance efforts, and the establishment of continuous dialogue mechanisms, organizations can successfully foster and sustain trust within multi-generational workforces. This ongoing nurturing of trust ensures that teams remain harmonious, productive, and resilient against challenges that may arise because of generational differences.

The following activities foster a trusting environment where team members feel valued, understood, and connected, facilitating better collaboration and productivity in a multi-generational team setting. Adapt and choose activities that best suit the needs and preferences of your team.

Group Activities

1. Icebreaker Questions

   Objective: Get to know each team member on a personal level.

   Activity: Begin meetings with each member answering a question, like a favorite book, hobby, or a fun fact about themselves.

   Benefit: Encourages sharing and fosters a personal connection between team members.

2. Workshops on Generational Differences

   Objective: Understand and appreciate the diverse perspectives within the team.

   Activity: Conduct workshops where team members can learn about the work habits, communication styles, and values of different generations.

   Benefit: Increases understanding and reduces generational stereotypes and biases.

3. Team-Building Outdoor Activities

   Objective: Build trust through shared experiences.

   Activity: Organize outdoor activities such as hiking, a ropes course, or a team sport. Choose activities that are accessible to all team members.

   Benefit: Facilitates communication, collaboration, and trust through shared challenges and experiences.

4. Problem-solving Challenges

Objective: Enhance team collaboration and communication.

Activity: Engage the team in problem-solving challenges or escape room activities where they have to work together to find solutions.

Benefit: Encourages the team to trust each other's skills and judgments.

5. Book Club

Objective: Foster deeper discussions and sharing of perspectives.

Activity: Create a book club where team members read and discuss books related to their industry, teamwork, or personal development.

Benefit: Encourages learning, sharing of ideas, and building connections beyond work-related topics.

6. Regular Check-Ins and Feedback Sessions

Objective: Open channels of communication and understanding.

Activity: Schedule regular one-on-one or team check-ins for sharing feedback and discussing any challenges faced by team members.

Benefit: Promotes an environment of openness and continuous improvement.

7. Volunteering Together

Objective: Building trust while contributing to a cause.

Activity: Organize volunteering activities that allow team members to contribute to a community or cause together.

Benefit: Fosters a sense of shared purpose and teamwork outside the work environment.

8. Workshops on Effective Communication

Objective: Improve communication skills within the team.

Activity: Conduct workshops focused on improving communication skills, such as active listening and giving and receiving feedback.

Benefit: Enhances mutual understanding and reduces misunderstandings within the team.

9. Celebrating Milestones and Successes

Objective: Recognize and appreciate team members' contributions.

Activity: Celebrate project milestones, team achievements, or personal successes of team members.

Benefit: Builds a sense of appreciation and belonging within the team.

Chapter 5:

Mentoring and Reverse

Mentoring

Traditional mentoring is a familiar concept where a more experienced professional (the mentor) guides, advises, and supports a less experienced individual (the mentee) in their personal and professional development. This form of mentoring aligns well with a hierarchical organizational structure, where wisdom trickles down from senior to junior members, cultivating a lineage of expertise and organizational knowledge.

Reverse mentoring flips this model on its head. In this innovative approach, younger employees mentor senior team members, bringing fresh perspectives, technological prowess, and contemporary market understandings to the forefront of organizational strategy and culture. Reverse mentoring facilitates a two-way street of learning, allowing a cross-pollination of skills, ideas, and insights that enrich the entire organizational ecosystem.

In a multigenerational workforce, the objectives of these mentoring models are multiple. They bridge the generational gap by fostering relationships built on mutual respect, learning, and shared objectives. These mentoring relationships serve as a conduit for knowledge sharing, skill enhancement, and cultural evolution within the organization.

The significance of mentoring in a multigenerational workforce lies in its ability to facilitate the flow of diverse ideas and to smooth out the edges of generational differences. Mentoring provides a scaffold for building relationships, developing a common language, and cultivating shared objectives. Both traditional and reverse mentoring have the power to allow every individual to feel valued and empowered to contribute to their fullest potential, leveraging their unique generational strengths.

5.1 Benefits of Traditional Mentoring

Experience Sharing: Traditional mentoring allows for a rich sharing of experience. Mentors can impart wisdom, share lessons learned over the years, and provide practical insights that textbooks and formal training might not cover.

Guidance: Mentors serve as a guide, helping mentees handle the challenges and uncertainties in their career paths. They can offer advice on professional development, decision-making, and problem-solving.

Support and Encouragement: A mentor often plays the role of a supporter and encourager, providing motivation, boosting confidence, and helping mentees believe in their capabilities.

Challenges in Traditional Mentoring and Overcoming Them

Generational Gap: Differences in values, communication styles, and technological adeptness between the mentor and mentee can pose challenges. Encouraging open-mindedness, empathy, and mutual understanding can help in bridging this gap.

Time Constraints: Both mentors and mentees often face time constraints. Clear expectations, regular check-ins, and mutual commitment to the process can help both mentors and mentees manage the challenge of time constraints.

Over-dependency: There might be a risk of mentees becoming overly dependent on their mentors. Promoting a sense of autonomy, encouraging problem-solving skills, and ensuring that mentees are active participants in the mentoring process can lessen this risk.

Relevance: Ensuring that the advice and guidance provided by the mentor remain relevant and adaptable to current workplace realities and challenges is essential. Continuous learning, staying updated with industry trends, and adaptability by the mentor are crucial.

5.2 Reverse Mentoring: A Two-Way Street

Reverse mentoring flips the script on traditional mentoring, encouraging individuals from older generations to learn from their younger counterparts. In this symbiotic relationship, junior employees become mentors, sharing their unique insights, fresh perspectives, and technological expertise with senior professionals who assume the role of the mentees. This role-reversal fosters an environment of reciprocal learning and mutual respect, enabling both parties to benefit from each other's strengths and perspectives.

Bridging Generational Gaps

Reverse mentoring stands as a powerful tool for bridging generational gaps within the workplace. By fostering relationships between different age groups it facilitates a two-way exchange of ideas, knowledge, and experiences. Such interactions can dismantle stereotypes, reduce biases, and promote a better understanding among diverse age groups. It encourages senior employees to view issues from a fresh perspective and adapt to new methodologies and technologies, enhancing their ability to communicate and collaborate effectively with younger team members.

Advantages of Reverse Mentoring

Tech-Savviness: Younger mentors, often more fluent in contemporary technologies and digital trends, can guide older professionals through the latest in technological advancements, social media, and digital tools. This transfer of knowledge helps the organization stay up-to-date and competitive.

Fresh Perspectives: Young mentors bring new ideas, innovative solutions, and a different worldview. Their fresh perspectives can be a catalyst for change and innovation, encouraging the organization to evolve and adapt to contemporary challenges and opportunities.

Fostering Inclusivity: Reverse mentoring fosters a culture of inclusivity and mutual respect. It allows for the recognition of the value that each generation brings to the table, promoting a sense of belonging and appreciation among all employees, regardless of their age.

Enhancing Adaptability: By exposing older workers to new ideas and approaches, reverse mentoring enhances their adaptability and resilience, essential traits in the ever-changing business landscape.

5.3 Building Successful Mentoring Relationships

Key Elements of Effective Mentoring

Effective mentoring, whether traditional or reverse, revolves around several fundamental elements that form the foundation of a successful mentoring relationship. These core components include mutual respect, active listening, openness to feedback, clear communication, and goal setting.

Mutual Respect: Respect forms the bedrock of any mentoring relationship. Both mentor and mentee should appreciate each other's experiences, values, and viewpoints, fostering a relationship built on trust and esteem.

Active Listening: A significant part of mentoring involves listening intently and empathetically. Mentors and mentees must be present, engaged, and receptive during their interactions, promoting a sense of value and understanding.

Openness to Feedback: Both parties should be open to giving and receiving constructive feedback. A willingness to learn and improve, coupled with a supportive and guiding approach, enhances the growth and development arising from the mentoring process.

Clear Communication: Open lines of communication facilitate the effective exchange of ideas, expectations, and feedback. Transparency and honesty should characterize interactions, ensuring that both parties are on the same page regarding objectives and progress.

Goal Setting: Establishing clear, measurable goals gives direction to the mentoring relationship. Goals should be realistic yet challenging, providing a roadmap for development and achievement.

Strategies for Promoting Successful Mentoring Relationships

Regular Meetings: Scheduling regular check-ins or meetings helps in maintaining the momentum of the mentoring relationship. It ensures continuous learning, feedback, and adjusting goals and strategies as required.

Setting a clear agenda for each meeting ensures that time is used effectively. It allows for the systematic coverage of topics, discussions, and feedback sessions, fostering structured progress.

Flexibility: Adaptability is essential to mentoring relationships. Be prepared to adjust goals, strategies, and schedules based on evolving needs, challenges, and opportunities.

Addressing and Overcoming Common Obstacles

Mismatched Expectations: Ensure that both mentor and mentee have aligned expectations. To prevent misunderstandings, it is important for both mentor and mentee to have open discussions about goals, roles, and expectations at the onset.

Time Constraints: Time management is crucial. Both parties should commit to dedicating sufficient time and effort to the mentoring process to ensure its effectiveness and success.

Maintaining trust and openness in the relationship requires us to treat matters discussed during mentoring sessions with confidentiality.

5.4 Case Studies: Success Stories of Mentoring and Reverse Mentoring

In this section, we will present real-life examples that illuminate the powerful impact of mentoring and reverse mentoring in organizations. These narratives will unravel the strategies, challenges, and triumphs encountered, offering valuable insights into the practical implementation and benefits of these mentoring approaches.

Traditional Mentoring: Nurturing Future Leaders

Consider the case of a senior executive who took under his wing a young, enthusiastic newcomer, guiding her through the organizational maze. With his rich reservoir of experience, the mentor helped nurture the professional development of the mentee, enabling her to manage challenges with increased confidence and competence. The mentor's guidance empowered the young professional to accelerate her learning curve, avoiding potential pitfalls and making significant contributions to the team's objectives. Through this supportive relationship, the mentee emerged as a future leader armed with a deeper understanding of organizational dynamics and enhanced decision-making skills.

Reverse Mentoring: Bridging the Digital Divide

An innovative tech startup employed reverse mentoring to bridge the technological and digital gaps within their team. The tech startup utilized reverse mentoring to pair a digitally savvy Gen Z employee with a senior leader, fostering a knowledge-sharing relationship. Through this exchange, the senior leader gained valuable insights into the latest technological trends, social media strategies, and digital tools that enhanced operational efficiency and customer engagement. On the flip side, the younger mentor benefited from the seasoned leader's strategic insight, absorbing lessons in leadership, decision-making, and organizational vision. This symbiotic relationship facilitated a two-way knowledge flow, fostering mutual growth and understanding.

Best Practices and Lessons Learned

Mutuality: Both mentors and mentees contribute valuable perspectives and knowledge, building successful mentoring relationships on mutual respect and learning. Both parties bring valuable perspectives and knowledge to the table, enriching the interaction.

Adaptability: Mentoring relationships should be fluid and adaptable, open to evolving based on the unique needs, challenges, and opportunities encountered by the mentor and mentee.

Structured Approach: Having a structured approach, including regular meetings, goal setting, and progress tracking, enhances the effectiveness and directionality of the mentoring process.

Open Communication: Fostering an environment where open, honest communication is encouraged facilitates a transparent exchange of ideas, feedback, and guidance.

By scrutinizing these case studies and the lessons they contain, we can gain practical knowledge that can guide the development, execution, and improvement of mentoring and reverse mentoring programs within our organizations. The valuable insights from these success stories act as a guide, helping to create successful mentoring relationships based on mutual respect, shared benefits, and common growth.

Chapter 6:

Flexible Work Arrangements

The Evolving Workplace

In a world where change is the only constant, the traditional paradigms of the workplace have been undergoing a remarkable transformation. A pivotal aspect of this transformation is the rising prevalence of flexible work arrangements, a revolutionary concept that is reshaping the contours of organizational structures and work processes. This flexibility manifests in various forms, such as remote working, flexible hours, and job sharing, among others, and heralds a new era of work-life integration.

Flexible work options are a considerate way to address the various needs and preferences of a workforce that includes different generations. Each generation, with its unique set of expectations, aspirations, and life stages, seeks a working environment that resonates with its specific needs. For instance, while a Baby Boomer might value opportunities for phased retirement and part-time engagement, a Millennial might seek flexibility to balance familial responsibilities, and a Gen Z employee might cherish the autonomy to work from anywhere, leveraging technological connectivity.

Organizations can effectively meet the varying needs of employees from different generations by adopting flexible work schedules, making the workplace more welcoming, understanding, and adaptable to employee requirements. Such flexibility not only enhances employee satisfaction and well-being but also fosters a culture of creativity, innovation, and productivity. In the subsequent sections, we will explore the various dimensions of flexible work arrangements, their impacts, and strategies for effective implementation of work policies that align well with the diverse ages and experiences of today's workforce. We will discover the many benefits of having flexible work arrangements.

6.1 Types of Flexible Work Arrangements

In the modern workplace, a multitude of flexible work arrangements flourish, each offering unique advantages catering to the diverse needs of a multigenerational workforce. In this section, we will explore various types of flexibility, focusing predominantly on remote work and flexible hours.

Remote Work

The concept of remote work has surged in prominence, allowing employees the freedom to execute their tasks from home or alternative locations outside the traditional office environment. Remote work stands as a pivotal arrangement that has shown a significant impact on many aspects, such as productivity, work-life balance, and the overall dynamics within teams comprising various generations.

Let's dissect the benefits and considerations essential to maximizing the potential of remote work:

Productivity: When relieved from the constraints of a formal office setting and the daily commute, many employees exhibit increased focus and productivity. However, the influence of remote work on productivity can fluctuate based on generational preferences and individual adaptability to this modality of work.

Work-Life Balance: Remote work can usher in a newfound sense of balance between professional obligations and personal life. The flexibility to tailor one's environment and schedule fosters a holistic approach to work, which can be appealing across different generational spectrums, each bringing their own values and needs to the forefront.

Team Dynamics: Team interactions and collaborations undergo a transformation with remote work. Strategies to maintain robust communication, foster team cohesion, and adapt to the challenges of virtual collaboration become paramount, necessitating an understanding of the varying comfort and proficiency levels across generations.

Flexible Hours

Flexible hours allow for a more adjustable daily schedule, giving employees the freedom to start and finish their work at different times. This approach supports individual schedules and personal life responsibilities, offering a kind of flexibility that is valuable to employees of all ages and backgrounds.

Accommodating Diverse Lifestyles and Preferences: Flexible hours show a workplace values diversity, considering not just the age differences but also the various lifestyles and outside responsibilities of employees. This flexibility lets each person tailor their work hours to fit their individual needs and preferences, promoting a feeling of independence and respect.

Impact on Team Collaboration and Coordination: Flexible hours indicate a workplace appreciates diversity, considering not only different ages but also the varied lifestyles and commitments of employees. This adaptability allows everyone to adjust their work schedules based on their unique needs and preferences, enhancing feelings of autonomy and respect.

Job Sharing: Job sharing is an innovative work arrangement where two employees collaboratively shoulder the responsibilities of a single full-time position, each bringing their unique skills and perspectives to the role. This model fosters diversity and flexibility within the workplace, facilitating a balance between professional commitments and personal life. Within a multigenerational context, job sharing can be particularly enriching, enabling a cross-pollination of experiences and insights across different age groups. This allows for a rich exchange of ideas, combining the experience of older generations with the new ideas and tech-savviness of the younger counterparts. Thus, job sharing can act as a conduit for mutual learning and adaptability, resonating with the diverse preferences and strengths of a multigenerational workforce.

As we explore various flexible work options, we will discuss how each type affects different people and aspects to consider. Adjusting these flexible options to meet the specific characteristics and needs of a workforce of various ages will be a key topic of our discussion.

6.2 The Impact of Flexibility on Different Generations

This section presents the various impacts of flexible work arrangements across different generational cohorts, highlighting the unique benefits and challenges encountered by each.

Baby Boomers: Often viewed as the traditionalists in the workforce, Baby Boomers might initially find the shift towards flexible work arrangements challenging. However, the option of flexible hours can be quite appealing to them, especially those eyeing retirement and looking to reduce work hours gradually. Remote work might also offer them an opportunity to cut down on commute times, enhancing work-life balance.

Generation X: For Gen X, often juggling family and work responsibilities, flexible work arrangements can be a significant boon. Remote work or flexible hours can allow them to manage their time effectively, aligning work commitments with personal obligations. This approach can enhance productivity and job satisfaction among Gen X employees.

Millennials: Accustomed to leveraging technology and valuing work-life integration, Millennials are likely to embrace flexible work arrangements enthusiastically. Such flexibility aligns with their preference for autonomy, enabling them to work in rhythms that suit their lifestyles and productivity cycles best, whether it be from home or a coffee shop.

Generation Z: As digital natives, Gen Z might find remote work to be second nature, comfortably using digital platforms and virtual collaborations. However, because they are in the early stages of their careers, thoughtful strategies should be in place to ensure they receive adequate mentorship and opportunities for professional development, even in remote or job-sharing scenarios.

Each generation's response to flexibility is different, necessitating organizations to be mindful and adaptive, ensuring that employing flexible work arrangements is individualized. Tailoring approaches to meet the specific needs and preferences of each generation is key to harnessing the full potential of flexibility in fostering a vibrant and productive multigenerational workforce.

6.3 Implementing Flexible Work Policies

Creating and implementing flexible work policies is a strategic process that requires thoughtful planning and execution. The goal is to foster an environment that promotes flexibility while maintaining a strong sense of accountability, productivity, and team cohesion.

Creating Policies: Begin by clearly defining what flexibility means within the context of your organization. Outline the different options available, such as remote work, flexible hours, and job sharing. Ensure that the policies are comprehensive, covering various aspects such as eligibility, scheduling, and expectations related to job performance and availability.

Communication: Keep communication clear and open to ensure everyone understands their roles and expectations. It's important to clearly communicate expectations to each team member and share the available flexible work options. Use communication tools that make sharing information easy to encourage teamwork and understanding.

Team Collaboration: Encourage teamwork and cooperation, even if team members aren't always physically present in the office. Use tools and technologies that help team members work together, share ideas, and stay connected, no matter where they are located.

Maintaining a Sense of Community: When putting flexible work policies into action, keeping a strong company culture and community feel is important. Make chances for team members to get to know each other, share, and build strong connections, whether in online meetings, team activities, or sometimes meeting in person.

Monitoring and Evaluation: Continuously monitor and evaluate the effectiveness of the flexible work policies. Seek feedback from employees to understand what works well and areas that might need adjustment or improvement.

Implementing flexible work policies requires a balance, ensuring that the organization's objectives are met while providing employees with the flexibility to manage their work in ways that align with their needs and preferences. These guidelines create a framework that supports successful implementation, promoting a happy, engaged, and productive workforce.

6.4 Managing and Leading Flexibly

In a world where flexible work arrangements are becoming the norm, leadership strategies must evolve to manage a team effectively under varied work setups. It requires a detailed approach that is anchored in empathy, trust, and clear communication.

Leadership Strategies: Managing a team flexibly necessitates leaders to be adaptable and open-minded. Strategies include setting clear expectations, defining roles and responsibilities, and establishing parameters for accountability and performance. Promoting a culture where quality and productivity are valued requires a focus on outcomes rather than hours spent working.

Empathy: Leaders should cultivate empathy, striving to understand each team member's unique circumstances, needs, and challenges. It involves being receptive to employees' concerns and feedback, and being supportive and compassionate in addressing any issues or obstacles they may face in their work arrangements.

Trust: Building trust is fundamental in a flexible work environment. Leaders should show trust in their team's ability to fulfill their responsibilities diligently, even when not physically present in the office. It involves giving autonomy, encouraging initiative, and valuing each person's contributions to the team's goals.

Clear Communication: Effective communication is pivotal in managing a team with varied work arrangements. Leaders should ensure that communication lines are always open, encouraging team members to share their thoughts, ideas, and progress. Facilitating regular check-ins, updates, and team meetings, whether virtual or in-person, is crucial for leaders to foster connection, collaboration, and a shared sense of purpose.

Managing and leading flexibly is about creating a supportive environment where each team member feels valued, connected, and motivated, irrespective of their work arrangement. It requires a leadership style that is both strategic and human-centric, promoting a culture of inclusivity, innovation, and shared success.

6.5 Measuring the Success of Flexible Work Arrangements

To ensure that flexible work arrangements are effective and beneficial, organizations must undertake a comprehensive assessment of their impact on team performance, employee satisfaction, and overall business success.

Assessing Team Performance: A crucial aspect involves evaluating how flexible work arrangements impact the productivity and output of teams. Project completion rates, quality of work, and adherence to deadlines can aid in evaluations. It is important to examine the ability of teams in a flexible setup to collaborate, communicate, and maintain cohesiveness.

Employee Satisfaction: Gauging employee satisfaction is vital in understanding the success of flexible work policies. Surveys, interviews, and regular check-ins can help to gather feedback from employees about their experiences, challenges, and the impact of flexible arrangements on their work-life balance and job satisfaction.

Overall Business Success: We should not overlook the broader impact on business objectives and outcomes. Assessing whether flexible work arrangements contribute to or hinder the achievement of business goals, client satisfaction, and competitive positioning is essential.

Continuous Improvement: Based on the assessment, organizations should be prepared to make necessary adjustments and improvements to their flexible work policies. This may involve tweaking the arrangements, offering additional support, or addressing any identified challenges or gaps.

Adaptation of Flexible Policies: A repeating approach that allows for the continuous adaptation and optimization of flexible work policies based on evolving needs, feedback, and business objectives is advisable. This promotes a culture of agility, responsiveness, and continuous enhancement.

Evaluating the success of flexible work arrangements involves a multifaceted analysis that is focused not just on quantitative outcomes, but also on the qualitative experiences of employees. A commitment to continuous assessment, learning, and adaptation is key to ensuring that flexible work policies are sustainable, effective, and mutually beneficial for both the employees and the organization.

Chapter 7:

Generational Learning Styles

In this chapter, we'll look at how different generations prefer to learn at work. People from different age groups have different ways they like to learn because of their unique life experiences and backgrounds. It's important for workplaces to recognize and adapt to these different learning styles. Doing this helps to keep all employees productive and engaged in their work. We'll explore these different learning styles and discuss how to create learning strategies that work well for everyone in the workplace.

7.1 Defining the Generational Learning Styles

In this section, we will define the preferred learning styles of different generations.

Baby Boomers: Baby Boomers prefer learning in a formal and structured way. They value learning from experts with a lot of experience. They often like traditional learning settings, such as classrooms and lectures.

Generation X: People in Generation X often prefer to learn on their own. They like a mix of both formal learning, like courses, and informal learning, like job experiences or discussions.

Millennials: Millennials often prefer learning that uses technology. They like to learn in ways that are flexible and that let them work with others. This group commonly used online courses, apps, and collaboration tools.

Generation Z: Generation Z is very comfortable using technology for learning. They prefer learning resources they can use anytime, like online videos or interactive apps. They like learning that is engaging and not just about listening or reading.

7.2 The Role of Technology in Learning

This section will explore the utilization of technology in learning and its impact on various generations.

Each generation's preferred learning style can be matched by utilizing technology in multiple ways. For example, those who prefer to learn anytime and anywhere can use online courses and videos.

Benefits: Technology can make learning more accessible. It can offer more ways to learn and can make learning more interesting.

Challenges: Using technology can also have problems. Some people might find it hard to use. There might be too many tools and platforms, making it confusing. There can also be issues like bad internet connections or systems not working properly.

7.3 Customizing Learning Approaches

This section focuses on how to tailor learning programs to meet the various needs and likes of a multigenerational workforce.

Strategies for Personalizing Learning: For effective learning, it's crucial to customize the approaches. Offering a variety of learning materials, such as videos, articles, and interactive sessions, can cater to different preferences. Providing options for when and how learning can happen—like self-paced online modules or scheduled live sessions— gives more choice and control to learners.

Learning Management Systems (LMS): LMSs play a significant role in personalizing learning. They allow the creation of customized learning paths. Users can choose what they want to learn based on their needs and interests. LMSs can also track progress and adapt based on the learner's performance and feedback, ensuring that learning is always relevant and targeted to everyone's needs.

7.4 Promoting Collaborative Learning

This section discusses creating a learning environment that encourages cooperation between different generations.

Benefits of Collaborative Learning: Encouraging a collaborative environment allows generations to learn from each other. It brings varied perspectives and experiences into the learning process, which can lead to richer and more comprehensive learning outcomes.

Facilitating Mentorship Programs: Mentorship programs, where experienced workers are paired with newer ones, can be very beneficial. They allow direct transfer of knowledge and skills, providing a valuable resource for newer workers and a sense of contribution and value for the more experienced.

Group Projects and Cross-Generational Forums: Including group projects and forums in learning programs can promote cross-generational interactions. These platforms allow for sharing of different viewpoints and knowledge, promoting a broader understanding and appreciation of various perspectives and approaches.

7.5 Overcoming Resistance to New Learning Methods

This section discusses strategies to increase acceptance and use of new learning methods across different age groups.

Encouraging Adoption of New Learning Platforms: For any new learning method to be effective, it first has to be accepted and used by the learners. Strategies that could help include making the new platforms user-friendly, providing necessary training and support, and communicating the benefits clearly to encourage the users to change.

Promoting a growth mindset fosters a culture where employees are encouraged to learn continuously and view challenges as opportunities to grow, which can help reduce resistance to new learning methods. When employees believe they can develop new skills and improve with effort and perseverance, they are more likely to embrace new learning methods and platforms.

Promoting a Continuous Learning Culture can also help in overcoming resistance by encouraging a learning environment where employees feel that their growth is valued and continuous learning is supported and rewarded. This could involve providing opportunities for professional development, recognizing and rewarding learning and improvement, and integrating learning into the organizational culture and daily workflows.

7.6 Measuring the Effectiveness Strategies

To ensure that learning strategies are effective and meet the objectives, it's important for organizations to assess their impact and outcomes. Here's how organizations can do this:

Using Feedback Mechanisms: Collecting feedback from participants is crucial. Surveys, questionnaires, or direct interviews can gather responses about the learning experience. Feedback can provide insights into what works well and what areas need improvement or adjustment in the learning strategies.

Key Performance Indicators (KPIs): Quantitatively assessing the effectiveness of strategies can be done using KPIs. Some KPIs could include completion rates, assessment scores, and application of learned concepts in the workplace. These metrics can provide a measurable way to evaluate the success of learning initiatives.

Evaluating Learning Outcomes: Assess whether the learning strategies are meeting the desired outcomes. This could involve evaluating whether the learners have gained the knowledge and skills and can apply them practically in their roles.

To identify areas where the learning strategies can be improved, use the collected data and feedback. This could involve adjusting the content, format, or delivery methods to better meet the needs and preferences of the learners.

Chapter 8:

Leading in a Land of Many:

Adaptive Leadership for a

Multigenerational Team

This chapter will present the importance of adaptive leadership in managing a multigenerational team. The chapter will provide guidance on how to leverage the unique strengths and talents of each generation while addressing their individual needs and aspirations.

8.1 The Art of Adaptive Leadership

Adaptive leadership plays a critical role in managing the diverse needs of a multi-generational team effectively. It involves an evolved leadership style that is responsive, flexible, and uniquely tailored to meet the individual needs of each team member.

Understanding Individual Strengths and Weaknesses

Adaptive leadership requires a profound understanding of each team member's strengths, weaknesses, and motivations. This personalized understanding is crucial to navigate the complexities and diverse needs presented by a multi-generational workforce.

Flexibility and Responsiveness

It is not about mimicking a chameleon but being inherently responsive and adaptable to the continuously shifting dynamics and needs of a multi-generational team. The leader should adopt a detailed and considerate approach towards each team member's unique perspective and needs, recognizing them as individuals rather than mere representatives of their respective generations.

Recognizing Generational Variabilities

Leaders practicing adaptive leadership recognize and respect the generational variabilities in their teams. For instance, while many Millennials may prioritize work-life balance, it's not a universal preference, with some placing a higher priority on career progression. Similarly, dispelling common stereotypes is essential, such as the notion of Baby Boomers being resistant to change, when many are quite adaptive and willing to learn.

Balancing Divergent Needs

A balancing act is required of adaptive leaders to meet the divergent needs and preferences of their team members. For instance, Venter (2017) found that a Gen Z employee might prefer regular feedback, whereas a Baby Boomer might lean towards a higher autonomy in their work.

The art of adaptive leadership lies in the ability to adjust your leadership approach to fit the unique needs of each team member, considering their individual differences and generational backgrounds. This way, leaders can create a nurturing and respectful atmosphere that values everyone's diverse talents and inclinations within a team that includes members from various age groups, which improves the overall performance and harmony of the team.

8.2 Leveraging the Strengths of Each Generation

Effective team performance in a multi-generational workforce is enhanced by recognizing and capitalizing on the unique strengths each generation possesses. This section outlines these generational strengths and how an adaptive leader can strategically leverage them to benefit the team and foster a positive work environment.

Recognizing Generational Strengths

According to the Pew Research Center, Baby Boomers are often characterized by a robust work ethic and a sense of loyalty towards their organization (Fry, 2019). Their wealth of experience and dedication make them invaluable assets in maintaining organizational continuity and wisdom.

Gen X members typically exhibit traits of self-reliance and rationality. Their ability to work independently and their practical approach to problem-solving are essential in driving teams towards realistic and effective solutions.

Millennials bring to the table tech-savviness, adaptability, and a value for diversity (Bourke & Dillon, 2018). Their comfort with technology and ability to adapt to changing circumstances can help to keep the team dynamic and open to new perspectives and innovations.

Gen Z individuals, being digital natives, are entrepreneurial and socially conscious (Francis & Hoefel, 2018). Their comfort with digital technologies and a mindset oriented towards social impact and entrepreneurship infuse the team with innovative ideas and approaches.

Strategic Leveraging of Strengths by Adaptive Leaders

Adaptive leaders have the role of strategically leveraging these diverse generational strengths collectively to benefit the team. For instance, pairing a Baby Boomer's extensive experience with a Gen Z's technological prowess in a mentorship program creates a symbiotic relationship that enhances both individuals' skills and knowledge.

Similarly, the adaptive nature of Millennials can help to navigate unforeseen challenges, ensuring that the team remains resilient and capable of adjusting to evolving scenarios. In contrast, Gen X members' pragmatic nature ensures that the team remains focused and grounded in practical realities, approaching objectives with balance and realism.

Leveraging the strengths of each generation requires a strategic and adaptive leadership approach that fosters an environment where each generation's unique capabilities are recognized and used effectively. By doing so, leaders can cultivate a harmonious and productive team dynamic that capitalizes on the diverse range of strengths and perspectives inherent within a multi-generational workforce.

8.3 Addressing the Unique Needs and Aspirations of Each Generation

Effective leadership in a multi-generational workforce involves acknowledging and addressing the distinctive needs and aspirations of each generation. Understanding these varied preferences and expectations is crucial to enhancing job satisfaction, productivity, and retention rates among team members.

Understanding Generational Needs and Aspirations

Baby Boomers often lean towards valuing job security and personal accomplishments in their professional lives (Fry, 2019). They find satisfaction in loyalty and long-term commitment to a single organization, seeking recognition for their dedicated service and achievements.

Gen X members prioritize work-life balance and job flexibility. They value the ability to maintain a healthy balance between professional commitments and personal life, often seeking roles that offer flexibility in work arrangements.

Millennials are driven by a sense of purpose in their work and opportunities for personal development and growth. They seek roles that allow them to contribute positively and grow professionally, valuing continuous learning and development (Bourke & Dillon, 2018).

Gen Z individuals value stability, an opportunity to make a social impact, and the formation of authentic connections in their professional environment. They seek roles in organizations where they feel a sense of stability and opportunities to contribute positively to societal challenges (Francis & Hoefel, 2018).

Strategies for Addressing Generational Needs

Leaders can employ various strategies to meet these diverse needs and aspirations. For instance, to cater to Gen X and Millennial preferences, offering flexible work arrangements such as remote working or flexible hours can be highly effective.

For attracting and retaining Gen Z talent, organizations could incorporate mentorship programs and foster environments that allow them to make meaningful contributions to societal causes. This approach aligns with their desire for authentic connections and social impact.

More specific strategic possibilities:

1. Customized Professional Development

    Baby Boomers: Offer opportunities to share their expertise through mentoring or coaching roles, allowing them to leave a legacy of knowledge.

    Gen X: Provide advanced training programs that enable them to upskill, keeping them engaged and relevant.

    Millennials: Establish a continuous learning environment with various development programs, workshops, and online courses.

Gen Z: Offer platforms for them to learn from various industry experts and peers, enhancing their practical knowledge.

2. Effective Communication Channels

Baby Boomers: Prefer formal and structured communication, like emails and official meetings.

Gen X and Millennials: Value efficient and direct communication; platforms like Slack or Microsoft Teams can be effective.

Gen Z: Engage through visually appealing and interactive platforms, considering their preference for digital communication.

3. Flexible Benefits Packages

Baby Boomers: May appreciate health benefits and retirement plans.

Gen X: Might value paid time off, flexible schedules, or childcare support.

Millennials and Gen Z: Could appreciate student loan assistance or wellness programs.

4. Inclusive and Diverse Culture

Promote a culture where every generation feels their opinions are valued and considered.

Encourage cross-generational collaboration and idea-sharing.

5. Feedback Mechanisms

Implement regular feedback sessions where each generation can express their viewpoints and suggestions.

Use surveys or suggestion boxes for those who prefer anonymous feedback.

6. Recognition and Reward Systems

    Baby Boomers: Traditional recognition methods, such as awards or certificates.

    Gen X and Millennials: Public acknowledgment or additional responsibilities.

    Gen Z: Instant recognition, possibly through social platforms or team chats.

7. Team-Building Activities

    Organize team-building activities that cater to the interests of different generations, promoting collaboration and understanding.

8. Technological Adaptation

    Provide necessary training for older generations to feel comfortable with new technologies.

    Leverage the tech-savviness of younger generations to foster innovation and efficiency.

Implementing these strategies can help address the distinct needs of each generation, promoting a harmonious and productive work environment.

Adaptively addressing the unique needs and aspirations of each generation fosters an inclusive work environment where each member feels valued and understood. By implementing strategies aligned with these generational preferences, organizations can enhance overall job satisfaction and productivity, ensuring a cohesive and retention-friendly multi-generational workforce.

8.4 Case Studies of Successful Adaptive Leadership

Real-world case studies provide practical insights into how adaptive leadership functions in managing multigenerational teams successfully.

Google: Project Oxygen

Google, a leader in tech innovation, champions adaptive leadership through "Project Oxygen." This initiative focuses on improving management practices, making them more flexible and responsive to the team's diverse needs. Their research-driven approach has resulted in enhanced team performance and employee satisfaction by encouraging managers to adapt their leadership styles according to team requirements and individual needs (Garvin et al., 2013).

3M: Leadership Programs for Generational Diversity

By curating leadership programs that explicitly accommodate generational diversity, 3M has fostered an environment where innovation flourishes, and continuous growth is promoted. Their adaptive leadership strategies include creating inclusive platforms for knowledge sharing and idea generation that resonate with their diverse team members (3M, 2020).

Costco: Employee-Centric Adaptive Leadership

Costco, the retail giant, focuses on adaptive leadership that prioritizes employee satisfaction. Their approach adapts to the multifaceted needs of a multigenerational workforce, ensuring that everyone, from Baby Boomers to Gen Z, feels valued and understood. This strategy has cultivated a satisfied and motivated workforce, leading to high productivity and retention rates (Relihan, 2018).

Microsoft: Embracing Generational Strengths

Microsoft shows adaptive leadership by recognizing and leveraging the distinctive strengths of different generations. Their leadership style promotes cross-generational mentorship and collaboration, enhancing overall team creativity and problem-solving capabilities. This approach has led to the development of innovative products and solutions by harnessing the power of generational diversity (Microsoft 365 Team, 2019).

Salesforce: Continuous Learning and Feedback

Salesforce exemplifies adaptive leadership by promoting a culture of continuous learning and feedback. Leaders at Salesforce are encouraged to maintain open communication channels and regularly check in with team members of all generations. This leadership style, which promotes a culture of continuous learning and feedback, has facilitated a supportive environment where employees feel their contributions are recognized and valued.

By examining these case studies, adaptive leadership helps to harness the full potential of multigenerational teams, fostering environments where innovation, satisfaction, and productivity thrive.

8.5 Common Questions and Objections

Leaders often encounter questions or objections regarding the implementation of adaptive leadership in managing multigenerational teams. Addressing these questions directly helps in clearing doubts and offering a clearer perspective on adaptive leadership's effectiveness.

Balancing Multigenerational Needs

Question: "How can I balance the needs of different generations without favoring one over another?"

Response: Focus on treating every team member as an individual, rather than merely a representative of a particular generation. Create strategies that equally cater to the varying needs of each team member, ensuring no single group feels favored or neglected (Reynolds, A., & Lewis, D., 2018).

The Essence of Adaptive Leadership

Question: "Is adaptive leadership just about pleasing everyone?"

Response: Adaptive leadership is not about universally pleasing all team members. Instead, it is a focused approach aiming to recognize and cater to the diverse needs of a multigenerational team, promoting a harmonious and productive working environment (Ramalingam et al, 2020).

Preventing Confusion

Question: "Won't constant adaptation confuse my team?"

Response: Clear, consistent communication is key. Ensure that the team understands the reasons behind any adaptations in leadership style or strategy, making change smoother and less confusing. Openly sharing the rationale behind changes fosters an environment of transparency and understanding.

Maintaining Consistency

Question: "How do I maintain consistency in my leadership style when I am continuously adapting?"

Response: Adaptive leadership allows for a core set of leadership principles that remain constant, providing stability. The adaptations are subtle shifts in approach to meet the evolving needs of the team, not a complete overhaul of leadership style.

Ensuring Fairness

Question: "How do I ensure that my adaptive leadership approach is unbiased?"

Response: Focus on objective assessment and equal opportunity. Ensure that you make adaptations based on genuine team needs and individual merits, preventing any form of favoritism or bias.

Addressing these questions and objections allows leaders to gain a deeper, more detailed understanding of adaptive leadership, facilitating its effective implementation in managing multigenerational teams.

Below are some actions that leaders can employ to exercise adaptive leadership within multigenerational teams. Implementing these activities and actions fosters adaptive leadership, enhancing the effectiveness of multigenerational teams and ensuring a harmonious and productive work environment.

Activities for Multigenerational Teams

1. Cross-generational Mentorship Programs

   Purpose: Facilitate knowledge exchange and foster relationships across generations.

   Activity: Pair younger employees with more experienced ones for mutual mentoring. Allow the sharing of experiences and skills, where both parties can learn and benefit.

2. Workshop on Generational Diversity

   Purpose: Enhance understanding and appreciation of different generational perspectives.

   Activity: Conduct workshops where team members can share their generational experiences and viewpoints, enabling others to gain insights and develop empathy.

3. Team-Building Exercises

   Purpose: Foster trust and improve communication among multigenerational team members.

   Activity: Organize team-building exercises and games that require collaboration and problem-solving, allowing team members to understand each other's strengths and working styles.

4. Roundtable Discussions

Purpose: Provide a platform for open communication.

We need to ensure that we organize sessions where team members can discuss their expectations, challenges, and suggestions, ensuring that each generation is heard and considered.

Actions and Knowledge for Leaders

1. Continuous Learning

    Action: Leaders should invest in continuous learning to stay updated with trends that apply to different generations.

    Knowledge: Understand the motivations, values, and communication styles of each generation.

2. Flexibility in Leadership Styles

    Action: Adapt leadership styles according to the needs and preferences of different generations within the team.

    Knowledge: Develop a sound understanding of various leadership styles and their effectiveness in different contexts.

3. Promoting Inclusivity

    Action: Encourage an inclusive environment where each generation feels valued.

    Knowledge: Recognize the common stereotypes and biases associated with different generations and actively work against them.

4. Tailoring Communication

    Action: Customize communication strategies to resonate with all team members, acknowledging different preferences and comfort levels with technology.

    Knowledge: Be well-versed in various communication tools and platforms, and understand how different generations prefer to communicate.

5. Conflict Resolution

    Action: Be proactive in identifying and resolving conflicts that may arise because of generational differences.

    Knowledge: Familiarize yourself with common points of contention among different generations and develop strategies to address them.

Chapter 9:

Shattering Glass Ceilings: Dispelling Biases and Stereotypes Across Generations

This chapter provides readers with a comprehensive understanding of common generational biases and stereotypes and equips them with practical tools to combat these harmful narratives in their workplaces.

9.1 Unveiling the Invisible: Understanding Generational Biases and Stereotypes

Generational biases and stereotypes often operate in the background, subtly influencing workplace dynamics and relationships. These biases, or subconscious beliefs, cause us to categorize individuals based on their age or generational group, affecting our interactions and expectations.

For example, people might commonly stereotype Baby Boomers as out of touch or resistant to change, while they might view Millennials as entitled or lacking loyalty to the workplace. People might primarily see Gen Z as tech-obsessed, overshadowing their other attributes and contributions.

Understanding these biases is the first step towards removing their impact. Recognizing that such stereotypes are oversimplified and often inaccurate representations of individuals is an essential step. It's crucial to challenge these biases, promoting a more individual understanding of each team member.

Here are a few strategies to combat generational biases and stereotypes:

The organization can conduct regular training sessions, workshops, or seminars to educate employees about the existence of these biases and stereotypes and their impact on the workplace.

Promote Individuality: Encourage team members to view each other as individuals with unique strengths, rather than mere representatives of their generational groups. Foster an environment where employees contributions are appreciated, regardless of the employee's age.

Encourage Intergenerational Collaboration: Facilitate projects or tasks that require collaboration among team members from various generational groups. This can help in breaking stereotypes as employees have time to get to know each other beyond generational labels.

Open Dialogue: Create platforms or forums where employees can openly discuss and share their experiences and viewpoints regarding generational biases, promoting empathy and understanding.

Incorporating these strategies can help in identifying and addressing the invisible barriers created by generational biases and stereotypes, fostering a more inclusive and harmonious workplace.

9.2 The Ripple Effect: The Impact of Biases and Stereotypes on Workplace Dynamics

Biases and stereotypes have a substantial, cascading effect on the workplace, influencing how team members interact, communicate, and collaborate. They plant seeds of miscommunication, misunderstanding, and conflict, thus disrupting the harmony and productivity of the work environment.

For instance, preconceived notions, leading to unfair treatment, can influence a Gen X manager who believes Millennials to be less committed, fostering resentment among team members. This type of bias diminishes morale, hinders cooperation, and creates a divisive atmosphere.

Biases and stereotypes obstruct the full utilization of a team's diverse skills and perspectives. When we allow stereotypes to influence our perceptions, we risk overlooking valuable contributions from various team members. A practical example would disregard an innovative idea from a Gen Z team member because of assumptions about their lack of experience or practical knowledge.

Such biases not only stifle individual expression and innovation but also inhibit the overall growth potential of the team. By undermining the unique strengths that each generation brings to the table, biases limit opportunities for collective learning and improvement.

In the broader perspective, these biases limit the overall ability of an organization to adapt, innovate, and remain competitive. Thus, recognizing and actively working to eliminate generational biases and stereotypes is crucial in fostering a dynamic, respectful, and highly productive multigenerational workplace. By doing so, we unlock the full range of talents, experiences, and perspectives that each generation offers, promoting a more enriched and effective organizational environment.

9.3 Mirror, Mirror on the Wall: Identifying Our Own Biases and Stereotypes

To manage a multigenerational workforce effectively, recognizing and addressing our own biases and stereotypes is crucial. Self-awareness serves as the foundation upon which we can begin dismantling these biases.

First, it's essential to identify and acknowledge our subconscious beliefs. For instance, if a Baby Boomer's proficiency with a new technology surprises us, it's an opportunity to recognize a bias about older generations being less tech-savvy. Such recognition is pivotal in understanding how these biases shape our interactions and decision-making processes.

Regular self-reflection and questioning of our assumptions are necessary tools for combating stereotypes. When we catch ourselves attributing a behavior or preference to a person based solely on their generational group—such as assuming a Gen Z employee prefers texting over face-to-face communication—it's imperative to pause and scrutinize this belief. Asking ourselves why we hold such an assumption and whether it's founded in reality or mere stereotype is a practical approach to dissecting and discarding biases.

The ongoing practice of self-examination helps to cultivate a more objective, respectful, and inclusive perspective. By continually challenging our biases, we open pathways to improved communication, collaboration, and understanding across generational divides in the workplace. This active engagement in introspection and improvement fosters a healthier, more harmonious, and productive work environment.

9.4 Breaking Down Walls: Practical Strategies to Overcome Biases and Stereotypes

Two studies, published in the Harvard Business Review (Rock & Grant, 2016; Ely & Thomas, 2020), converge on the idea that encouraging interaction among diverse group members—especially across different generations—significantly mitigates biases and enhances organizational dynamics. The findings suggest that fostering a collaborative environment where individuals from various age groups work together is an effective method to address age-related biases. This approach not only promotes a healthier, bias-reduced atmosphere but also bolsters creativity, team performance, and mutual understanding among team members.

Deloitte University's research offers pivotal insights into organizational innovation in relation to inclusive cultures. Their study reveals that organizations promoting inclusivity are six times more likely to be innovative. This inclination towards innovation arises from encouraging diverse cultures within the organization, allowing a mix of various viewpoints and ideas, which becomes a rich source of creativity and novel solutions (Bourke, 2016).

These studies collectively underscore the significance of inclusivity and diversity in fostering innovation and mitigating biases within organizational settings.

Dr. Leah Georges, a distinguished professor at Creighton University and an accomplished TEDx speaker, offers insightful perspectives on generational stereotypes in the workplace. In her notable presentation at TEDxCreightonU, titled "How Generational Stereotypes Hold Us Back at Work," Dr. Georges outlines the misconceptions often associated with generational stereotypes, revealing that such preconceived notions often disappear under scrutiny. She earnestly advocates for the encouragement of cross-generational conversations as a potent tool to dismantle these entrenched stereotypes, thereby facilitating a more harmonious and collaborative workplace environment.

Lindsey Pollak, a renowned expert and authoritative author on millennials, brings forth compelling viewpoints on leadership dynamics within multigenerational teams. In her groundbreaking work, *The Remix: How to Lead and Succeed in the Multigenerational Workplace*, Pollak stresses the importance of adapting leadership styles to align with the variety of age groups in modern workplaces. She suggests focusing on recognizing and valuing each person's unique strengths and abilities, rather than sticking to common misconceptions based on their age group. This helps create a workplace where people manage effectively, and individuals from different generations can work well together.

Through their respective works, both Dr. Georges and Lindsey Pollak emphasize the pivotal role of dissolving generational stereotypes to nurture a more inclusive and successful multigenerational workplace.

The Harvard Business Review published an article titled "Bridging Generational Divides in Your Workplace." The article emphasizes the need for businesses to adapt their diversity, equity, and inclusion strategies to account for an aging workforce. The authors suggest that leaders should focus on creating cultures of candor, inclusion, integrity, and innovation to power productivity into the future. They also highlight the benefits that come with an aging workforce and the demographic changes that organizations face today.

The Journal of Business and Psychology presents research that highlights the powerful influence of interactions between different age groups in reducing prejudice in the workplace. The study suggests that creating opportunities for collaboration among various age groups is essential for building a successful organizational culture. Purposeful interactions between different generations help lessen biases and stereotypes, creating a stronger and more inclusive workplace. This approach helps reduce age-related discrimination and prejudice.

Both journals stress the importance of promoting intergenerational interactions and knowledge sharing as a strategy to overcome stereotypes and foster a more inclusive and effective workplace.

A compelling report by Catalyst clearly shows how inclusive leadership can reduce biases and stereotypes in the workplace. Catalyst's detailed research explains how inclusive leadership can change organizational cultures, creating environments that are strong against biases and stereotypes. Inclusive leadership helps create a unified workplace where everyone feels included, and it steadily reduces the negative effects of biases (Prime & Salib, 2014).

McKinsey & Company, in their detailed analysis, highlight the important relationship between diversity, inclusivity, and better business results. Their reports strongly advocate for organizations to accept age diversity as a key organizational asset. It makes a strong case for recognizing the power of diversity in age in driving strong and innovative business performance. McKinsey's explanation stresses the transformational power of diversity and inclusion as essential elements for a lively and successful organizational model (Hunt et al., 2018).

Together, these organizational reports herald the significance of inclusive leadership and generational diversity as critical cornerstones for creating an organizational culture that is conducive to innovation, performance, and the diminution of biases and stereotypes.

To dismantle the barriers erected by biases and stereotypes within a multigenerational workforce, adopting various proactive strategies is essential. Here are some practical approaches and guidelines to foster a more inclusive and understanding workplace.

1. Open Communication

    It is fundamental to facilitate open dialogues where team members are encouraged to share their experiences and perspectives. For instance, organizing team meetings where individuals, such as Millennials, can openly discuss their work ethics and ambitions helps in debunking prevailing stereotypes, such as Millennials being entitled or apathetic.

2. Implicit Bias Workshops

    Exercise: Conduct workshops helping employees recognize and address their implicit biases.

Research Support: A study by Carnes et al., (2012), suggests that workshops on implicit biases can lead to increased awareness and a change in biases.

Action Steps:

Facilitate exercises that help participants identify their biases.

Promote discussion and reflection on how biases affect work relationships and decision-making.

3. Role-Playing Activities

Exercise: Engage teams in role-playing activities to understand different generational perspectives.

Expert Opinion: Dr. Stella Nkomo, a professor and researcher in the field of diversity management and leadership, has conducted extensive research on race and gender in organizations, leadership, and managing diversity. She recommends role-playing to increase empathy and understanding among diverse groups (Nkomo, 1996).

Action Steps:

Create scenarios based on common workplace situations.

Allow employees to role-play different generational perspectives.

4. Incorporate Diversity and inclusion in onboarding

Guideline: Make diversity and inclusion training an essential part of the onboarding process.

Research Support: A report by Deloitte shows that early D&I training can help to set the tone for an inclusive environment (Bourke & Dillon, 2018).

Action Steps:

Develop a module that introduces new employees to the company's commitment to generational diversity.

Highlight the value each generation brings to the organization.

5. Create Multigenerational Mentoring Programs

Guideline: Pair younger employees with more experienced ones to foster mutual understanding.

Expert Opinion: Audrey Murrell, Ph.D., suggests that mentoring can be a powerful tool to break stereotypes and foster inclusivity (Murrell, 2017).

Action Steps:

Facilitate formal mentor-mentee relationships focused on knowledge and experience sharing.

Ensure the structure and support of mentoring programs.

6. Regularly Update D&I Policies and Training

Make sure that you update policies and training programs regularly to reflect current best practices, as stated in the guideline.

Research Support: A 2018 McKinsey report emphasizes the importance of evolving diversity and inclusion (D&I) strategies to stay effective (Hunt et al., 2018).

Action Steps:

Continuously seek feedback from employees on D&I initiatives.

Stay informed about the latest research and best practices in diversity and inclusion.

7. Promote Inclusive Language

   Guideline: Encourage the use of language that is inclusive and not tied to specific age-related stereotypes.

   Expert Opinion: Jennifer Brown, an inclusive leadership expert, stresses the importance of language in fostering an inclusive environment (Brown, 2019).

   Action Steps:

   Offer training sessions on how language can exclude or include diverse groups.

   Encourage leaders to model inclusive language.

8. Leverage Technology for D&I

   Guideline: use technology to deliver customized D&I training and gather data on its effectiveness.

   Research Support: A PwC report suggests that technology can play a significant role in enhancing D&I initiatives (PwC, 2021).

   Action Steps:

   Explore online platforms that offer D&I training.

   Use data analytics to measure the impact of D&I initiatives.

9. Involve Leadership in D&I Initiatives

   Guideline: Ensure that organizational leaders are active participants and champions of D&I initiatives.

   Expert Opinion: Dr. Robert Livingston emphasizes the role of leadership in setting the tone for inclusivity in organizations (Livingston, 2021).

Action Steps:

Encourage leaders to participate actively in D&I training and initiatives.

Ensure that leadership communicates the importance of D&I to the organizational culture.

Dispelling biases and stereotypes necessitates a multi-pronged approach that involves continuous learning, reflection, and proactive strategies to foster an inclusive environment where diversity in all its forms, including generational, is celebrated and leveraged for organizational success.

By integrating these strategies into the organizational culture, we can promote a more enriched, empathetic, and fair work environment where each generation feels valued and understood. This approach not only helps in neutralizing biases and stereotypes, but also cultivates a fertile ground for innovation, collaboration, and mutual growth.

9.5 Case Studies: Successful Strategies in Dispelling Biases and Stereotypes

Various companies have successfully started practical strategies to tackle biases and stereotypes, fostering an environment of inclusivity and mutual understanding. Here are case studies from AT&T and Johnson & Johnson that show effective implementations of such strategies.

AT&T: Reverse Mentoring Program

AT&T introduced a reverse mentoring program, a novel initiative where executives are paired with younger employees to act as their mentors. This method helped remove stereotypes, promoting the sharing of views and encouraging a better mutual understanding between different age groups in the organization. It became a way for knowledge and insights to be exchanged, helping to get rid of existing biases related to age and job levels (Jackson, n.d.).

Johnson & Johnson: Generation Now

Johnson & Johnson created the Generational Resource Group to improve understanding and awareness of different age groups. The group's goal is to create a work environment where the diversity of generations is acknowledged and appreciated. By organizing activities and programs, the group actively works to increase understanding between different age groups, reduce biases, and encourage a united and collaborative work atmosphere (Johnson & Johnson, 2023).

These case studies reveal the powerful results of carefully planned strategies that remove biases and stereotypes in the workplace. These efforts not only break down the obstacles created by biases but also importantly, contribute to building a peaceful work environment where differences in age and experience are appreciated and used for shared progress and creativity.

Activities and exercises to help eliminate biases and stereotypes among different age groups in the workplace are below. Putting these activities into action will help create a more welcoming and empathetic work environment by reducing biases and stereotypes among various generations.

Group Activities

1. Story Sharing

    Objective: To allow individuals to share personal stories and experiences that defy stereotypes.

    Activity: Organize a session where team members from different generations share unique personal stories or experiences that helped shape their careers.

    Discussion: After each story, have a group discussion about any surprising elements or how the story challenges existing stereotypes.

2. Reverse Mentoring

    Objective: To facilitate mutual understanding and respect among generations.

    Activity: Pair younger employees with more experienced professionals. In this situation, both should benefit. The younger one learns from the experienced employee and the older employee learns new technologies from the younger employee.

    Discussion: Allow both parties to share what they learned and how their perceptions have changed.

3. Generational Interview

    Objective: To encourage cross-generational communication and understanding.

    Activity: Have team members from one generation interview a colleague from a different generation, focusing on work experiences, career paths, and the use of technology.

Discussion: Share interesting findings and commonalities discovered through the interviews.

4. Work Style Workshop

   Objective: To explore and appreciate different work styles across generations.

   Activity: Conduct a workshop where team members discuss their work styles, preferences, and what they find effective.

   Discussion: Identify common ground and unique strengths that each generation brings to the workplace.

5. Role-Playing Scenarios

   Objective: To empathize and understand different generational perspectives.

   Activity: Create scenarios that reflect generational stereotypes or biases, and have team members role-play these scenarios.

   Discussion: Debrief each role-play, discussing the feelings, misconceptions, and learnings from each scenario.

6. Bias Busting Workshops

   Objective: To educate employees about unconscious biases.

   Activity: Organize workshops that identify and tackle unconscious biases, promoting a more inclusive environment.

   Creating quizzes, surveys, or questionnaires to uncover unconscious biases involves asking questions that help participants reflect on their attitudes, behaviors, and decisions in various scenarios. We can include some examples of questions or prompts to help reveal biases.

Quizzes:

Scenario-Based Questions: Present a scenario and ask participants to choose an action or reaction. Their choices can reveal biases.

Example: "In a job interview, who are you more likely to consider a better fit? Candidate A who graduated from an Ivy League but seems reserved, or Candidate B who is from a lesser-known college but seems more personable?"

Surveys:

Rating Scales: Ask participants to rate statements to understand their leanings or preferences.

Example: On a scale of 1–5, how much do you agree with this statement: "Younger employees are more innovative and adaptable."

Questionnaires:

Reflection Questions: Open-ended questions for self-reflection.

Example: "Describe an instance where you felt uncomfortable working with someone from a different age group. What made you feel that way?"

Preference Questions: Asking about preferences in working styles or colleagues.

Example: "Do you feel more comfortable working with people of a similar age group? Why or why not?"

Decision-Making Questions: Asking about decision preferences in professional scenarios.

Example: "When assigning a leader for a new project, are you more inclined to choose someone with more experience, even if they lack some technical skills?"

Discussion: Encourage participants to share their thoughts and how they plan to apply what they've learned.

7. Roundtable Discussions

Objective: To foster open communication and idea sharing.

Conduct roundtable discussions where each generation is represented, discussing topics like technology, work-life balance, or career development.

Discussion: Highlight insights and suggestions that emerged from the discussion for improving the workplace.

8. Appreciation Sessions

Objective: To cultivate appreciation for diversity and various skills.

Activity: Organize sessions where team members express appreciation for a colleague from a different generation, mentioning specific qualities or contributions.

Discussion: Reflect on the value that generational diversity brings to the team and the broader organization.

Chapter 10:

Onboarding Techniques

Onboarding is a critical process that involves integrating new employees into the organization, familiarizing them with the company culture and expectations, and providing the tools and information needed to start their jobs effectively. It's not merely an initiation but a comprehensive experience that should make employees feel welcomed, valued, and prepared to contribute to the company's success.

An effective onboarding process holds significant importance in integrating employees of all ages into the organizational culture. It is especially crucial in a multigenerational workforce where different generations—Baby Boomers, Gen X, Millennials, and Gen Z— coexist. A well-structured onboarding plan can help in bridging generational gaps, promoting mutual understanding, and creating a cohesive work environment that leverages the diverse strengths of each generation. In this way, organizations can foster a harmonious atmosphere that facilitates collaboration, innovation, and productivity across all age groups.

10.1 Designing a Universal Onboarding Process

Creating an onboarding process that resonates with all generations is essential for fostering an inclusive workplace. The key components of such a universal onboarding process include clarity, communication, and continuous support.

Clarity: Begin with a clear introduction of the organization's vision, values, and expectations. Ensure that every new hire, regardless of generation, understands their role, responsibilities, and how they contribute to the overall organizational goals.

Communication: Establish open lines of communication. Make sure new employees feel comfortable asking questions and expressing their thoughts or concerns. Regular check-ins and updates are crucial to keeping everyone informed and engaged.

Continuous Support: Offer continuous support through resources, mentorship, and opportunities for professional development. We should provide necessary tools and information through training if needed.

By implementing a universal approach, the onboarding process becomes more accessible and beneficial for everyone, easing the transition for all new hires, irrespective of their generational classification. This approach promotes a sense of belonging, boosts morale, and facilitates a smoother adaptation to the company culture and workflow.

10.2 Tailoring the Onboarding Experience to Different Generations

An effective onboarding process also considers the unique needs and preferences of different generations. Customizing certain elements of the onboarding can make the experience more resonant and engaging for each group.

Baby Boomers: Baby Boomers often value structured, formalized training and clear guidelines. Including in-person orientation sessions, detailed handbooks, and opportunities for one-on-one interactions with team members and leaders can be effective.

Generation X: Generation X appreciates autonomy and efficiency. Providing them with a mix of traditional onboarding activities, opportunities to quickly dive into their roles, and the flexibility to learn at their own pace can be impactful.

Millennials: As digital natives, Millennials often thrive with technology-driven onboarding processes. Incorporating digital platforms, virtual tours, and online training modules can appeal to their tech-savvy nature. Millennials often value a company's culture and social responsibility, so highlighting these aspects during onboarding is crucial.

Generation Z: Being the youngest in the workforce, Generation Z might benefit from a more interactive and engaging onboarding process. Gamifying some aspects of the training, incorporating social media, and facilitating peer interactions can make the process more appealing.

Modifying activities and communications to align with each generation's preferences enhances their onboarding experience, promoting quicker and more effective integration into the workplace. Tailoring the approach ensures that each generation feels valued and understood from the outset, laying the foundation for a successful tenure at the organization.

10.3 Leveraging Technology in the Onboarding Process

In the modern workplace, technology plays a pivotal role in enhancing the onboarding experience. Using technological tools and platforms can streamline the process, making it more efficient and adaptable to the needs of different generations.

Onboarding Platforms: Various specialized onboarding platforms are available that guide new hires through necessary paperwork, training modules, and other initial tasks. These platforms centralize information and resources, making it easy for new hires to find what they need.

Learning Management Systems (LMS): LMS can deliver online training and resources to new hires. They offer flexibility, allowing new employees to access materials anytime and anywhere, which can be beneficial for remote workers.

Communication Tools: Tools like Slack, Microsoft Teams, or Google Workspace can facilitate communication and collaboration among new hires and existing team members. These tools also allow for instant communication, file sharing, and scheduling.

Video Conferencing: Platforms like Zoom or Microsoft Teams are valuable for virtual meet-and-greets, team introductions, and remote training sessions. They help in connecting remote employees and fostering a sense of team unity.

Feedback tools can incorporate technologies that allow new employees to give and receive feedback into the onboarding process. Regular feedback can help new hires adjust their strategies and improve their performance continually.

Leveraging these technological tools can make the onboarding process more dynamic, engaging, and responsive to the needs of a multigenerational workforce. They allow organizations to provide a comprehensive and flexible onboarding experience, improving the likelihood of new hire retention and success.

10.4 Mentorship and Peer Support During Onboarding

Mentorship and peer support are integral parts of the onboarding process, playing a crucial role in helping new hires of all ages integrate into the workplace smoothly and effectively.

Role of Mentorship: Having a mentor provides new employees with a go-to person for guidance, advice, and support as they navigate the early stages of their career within the organization. Mentors can offer valuable insights, answer queries, and help overcome challenges, facilitating a smoother adaptation process for the new hires.

Peer Support: New employees paired with peers have the advantage of receiving support from individuals who have recently experienced the onboarding process themselves. Peers can offer practical advice, social support, and help in day-to-day tasks and adjustments.

Fostering a Sense of Belonging: Mentorship and peer support contribute to creating a supportive and inclusive atmosphere. They help new hires feel valued and connected, fostering a sense of belonging and engagement with the team and the organization.

Customization Based on Generational Needs: We can tailor the mentorship and peer support strategies based on generational preferences and needs. For instance, while baby boomers might prefer formal mentorship structures, millennials and Gen Z might appreciate more informal, collaborative peer interactions.

Matching Strategies: We should consider how to match mentors and peers with new hires. Effective matching can enhance the quality of the support relationship, ensuring that new employees receive relevant and helpful guidance.

By leveraging mentorship and peer support during onboarding, organizations can facilitate the integration of new hires into the organizational culture, enhancing their initial experience and paving the way for their success and productivity within the team.

10.5 Continuous Improvement of Onboarding Strategies

Continuous evaluation and improvement are essential for keeping onboarding strategies effective and aligned with the evolving needs of a diverse, multigenerational workforce.

Importance of Evaluation: Regular assessment of onboarding processes ensures they meet the current needs and preferences of new hires. It helps in identifying areas of strength and pinpointing aspects that require enhancement or modification.

Using Feedback: Gathering feedback from new hires is a valuable source of insight for improving the onboarding process. Their experiences and perspectives can highlight what's working well and what isn't, providing direct pathways for improvement.

Change and adaptation: Based on the evaluation and feedback, necessary adjustments can be made to the onboarding strategies. This could involve updating technologies used, changing mentorship programs, or tailoring communication methods to better suit different generational needs.

Maintaining Relevance: Continuous improvement helps in ensuring that onboarding processes stay relevant and can effectively integrate new employees into the organization's culture and operations.

By dedicating attention to the continuous improvement of onboarding strategies, organizations can promote a positive initial experience for new hires, fostering their successful integration and longer-term satisfaction and productivity within the team.

10.6 Sample of Onboarding Strategies

Following is an example of a new employee orientation program designed specifically to address multi-generational employees.

Innovative Multigenerational New Employee Orientation Program

Company: XYZ Corp

Objective:

To implement an innovative New Employee Orientation Program that is particularly attuned to the diverse needs and expectations of a multigenerational workforce, ensuring a smooth and welcoming integration into the company's culture and operational processes.

Background:

Recognizing the challenges posed by a workforce composed of multiple generations (Boomers, Gen X, Gen Y, Gen Z), XYZ Corp committed to revamping its New Employee Orientation Program. The goal was to create an orientation experience that respects the varied expectations, learning styles, and career aspirations of different age groups, fostering a sense of belonging and engagement from day one.

Program Development:

Key stakeholders, including representatives from each generation, were engaged in the planning process to incorporate a diversity of perspectives and insights. The program was flexible, inclusive, and adaptable to cater to different learning preferences and technological proficiencies.

Program Components:

Welcome Session: A universal introduction to the company's mission, values, and organizational structure, ensuring that all employees, regardless of their generation, start with a foundational understanding of the company.

Customized Workshops: Tailored sessions addressing the specific needs and preferences of each generation. For example, hands-on tech tutorials for Boomers, career development paths for Gen X, work-life balance strategies for Gen Y, and rapid onboarding processes for Gen Z.

Mentorship and Networking: Establishing mentorship pairs or groups, encouraging cross-generational interaction and knowledge sharing. Networking events to promote intergenerational communication and team building.

Feedback Loops: Continuous improvement mechanisms like surveys and focus groups for new employees to share their orientation experiences, ensuring the program remains responsive to evolving needs.

Outcome:

XYZ Corp's innovative orientation program has received positive feedback from new hires across all generational groups. Employees report feeling more understood, valued, and integrated into the company culture, resulting in improved job satisfaction and productivity.

Enhanced Engagement: New hires reported a stronger sense of belonging and motivation, reducing initial turnover rates.

Improved Collaboration: The program has facilitated better cross-generational understanding and communication, enhancing team collaboration and productivity.

Positive Cultural Impact: By valuing and respecting the diverse needs of its multi-generational workforce from the outset, the company has fostered a more inclusive and harmonious workplace culture.

Lessons Learned:

Tailoring orientation content and approaches to different generational needs enhance engagement and satisfaction.

Involving representatives from each generation in the planning process ensures a more relevant and empathetic program.

Flexibility and adaptability are key to meeting the diverse needs of a multi-generational workforce.

XYZ Corp's multi-generational orientation program serves as an exemplary model of how thoughtful onboarding strategies can facilitate the successful integration of a diverse workforce, promoting a more inclusive, respectful, and productive organizational culture.

Chapter 11:

Decoding the Digital Divide: Bridging Tech Gaps Across Generations

The digital divide across generations is a significant challenge that can affect collaboration and productivity. However, with the right strategies and understanding, it can be bridged, fostering a more inclusive and efficient digital work environment.

11.1 Understanding the Digital Divide

The digital divide in the workplace refers to the gap between those who are adept and comfortable with technology and those who are not, and this can often align along generational lines. This divide can manifest itself in various aspects of work, particularly in communication and collaboration.

Communication Preferences:

Different generations have varied preferences for communication. Older generations, such as Baby Boomers and Gen X often lean towards more traditional forms of communication, such as emails or face-to-face meetings. In contrast, younger generations, like Millennials and Gen Z favor instant messaging platforms such as Slack or Asana, valuing speed and convenience.

Adaptability to Technology:

Younger generations usually exhibit a quicker adaptability to new technologies and digital platforms, embracing changes more readily. According to a 2019 report by the Pew Research Center, older generations may find it daunting to constantly adapt to the swift advancements in technology (Livingston, 2019).

Attitudes Towards Technology:

The digital divide also extends to the differing attitudes towards technology across generations. For digital natives like Gen Z, technology is a fundamental aspect of life and work. Conversely, Baby Boomers might perceive technology as a tool rather than an intrinsic element of their professional and personal lives.

Impact on Workplace Dynamics:

This generational digital divide can lead to misunderstandings and conflicts within the workplace. For example, there might be a divergence in the perception of efficiency and effectiveness, where a Gen Z might view a Baby Boomer's inclination for in-person meetings as less efficient, while the Baby Boomer might find an over-reliance on digital communication as lacking a personal touch.

Understanding these aspects of the digital divide is crucial for fostering a workplace environment where technology acts as a bridge rather than a barrier, promoting inclusivity and effective collaboration among all team members.

11.2 Strategies to Bridge the Digital Divide

Bridging the digital divide within a multigenerational workplace requires strategies that promote inclusivity, continuous learning, and open communication. Here are some effective strategies:

Promoting Continuous Learning:

Fostering a culture where continuous learning and adaptability are valued is essential. Providing regular training sessions which are designed considering various learning styles and technological know-how of different generations can make a significant difference. An example of this is Intel's reverse mentoring program, where younger employees assist older ones in navigating new technological tools (Together, n.d.).

Self-Paced Learning Resources:

Creating opportunities for self-paced learning is also a beneficial strategy. A notable example is Procter & Gamble, which offers an online learning portal. This portal includes tutorials on a range of digital tools, allowing employees to learn at their own pace and according to their comfort and proficiency levels.

Encouraging Open Communication:

Open communication about technological preferences, benefits, and challenges is central to bridging the digital divide. Discussions that facilitate a mutual understanding of various digital tools and their effectiveness can be very advantageous. Salesforce illustrates this approach by having a platform where employees can share experiences and offer suggestions concerning digital tools.

Addressing Concerns and Providing Support:

Understanding and addressing the technological concerns of all team members irrespective of their generation, is crucial. For example, while older employees might have reservations regarding the privacy aspects of certain digital platforms, the younger workforce might feel hindered by the slow adoption of innovative tools. Acknowledging and addressing these concerns fosters a respectful and supportive environment where each team member feels valued and heard.

11.3 Fostering a Technologically Inclusive Workplace

Creating a technologically inclusive workplace is a practical approach to bridging the digital divide across different generations. Here's how to foster an environment where each generation feels confident and competent in utilizing digital tools:

User-Friendly and Accessible Digital Tools:

Selecting digital tools that are intuitive and user-friendly is essential. These tools should cater to all, from tech-savvy individuals to those less acquainted with digital technologies. A great example of this inclusivity is Google Workspace, which offers a collection of tools that are easy to navigate, accommodating a broad spectrum of technological skills.

Providing Adequate Support and Resources:

Ensure that ample support and resources are available for all employees, facilitating their comfort and proficiency with various digital tools. IBM exemplifies this strategy by having a specialized IT support team readily available to assist employees with technological queries and challenges (IBM, 2020).

Valuing Unique Digital Strengths:

Recognize and appreciate the diverse digital strengths that each generation brings. Older employees often provide a cautious and analytical outlook when evaluating new technological tools, contributing to a balanced perspective on risks and benefits. In contrast, the younger workforce often introduces innovation and fresh ideas concerning technology usage. Both these viewpoints are vital in making well-rounded technological decisions in a workplace.

Leveraging the Diverse Strengths:

Using the varied digital capabilities of different generations enhances innovation and operational efficiency. Companies like Toyota have successfully harnessed the distinct technological strengths of various generations to bolster innovation and improve overall productivity.

Incorporating these strategies will nurture a technologically inclusive environment, encouraging collaboration, innovation, and a unified approach to achieving organizational objectives.

11.4 Success Stories of Overcoming the Digital Divide

Examining real-world examples offers practical insights into how various organizations have successfully bridged the digital divide. Here are a couple of cases where companies took initiatives to enhance the digital literacy of their multigenerational workforce:

Walmart's Digital Skills Training Program

Walmart, a notable retail giant, has proactively taken steps to improve the digital literacy of its workforce. The company has rolled out a digital skills training program, which has significantly improved digital literacy across all generational groups of its employees. This strategic initiative, highlighted in a 2019 report by Gartner, has made a considerable impact in leveling the technological playing field and promoting inclusivity (Gartner Research, 2019).

Bridging the digital divide is entirely workable with dedicated strategies and a commitment to promoting an inclusive environment. Such initiatives enhance collaboration, efficiency, and the overall technological adaptability of the entire workforce.

Practical exercises and activities to help bridge the tech gaps in a multigenerational team. Implementing a combination of these activities can promote tech proficiency, confidence, and cross-generational collaboration in using technology effectively in the workplace.

Group Activities

1. Technology Workshops

   Objective: To offer hands-on experience and guidance on various technologies.

   Activity: Conduct workshops where different generations can learn about the various tools and technologies essential for the workplace. Customize the pace and content according to the audience.

2. Peer Tutoring Sessions

   Objective: To promote peer-to-peer learning.

   Activity: Encourage employees to pair up with a colleague from another generation to teach or guide each other on using different tech tools or platforms.

3. Show and Tell

   Objective: To showcase the benefits and functionalities of different technologies.

   Activity: Organize sessions where team members can present a tech tool or software application that they find useful and show how they use it in their workflow.

4. Reverse Mentoring

   Objective: To allow younger employees to mentor older team members.

   Activity: Create pairs where a less experienced employee mentors a senior team member in understanding and adopting new technologies.

5. Tech Support Teams

   Objective: To offer continued tech support and guidance.

   Activity: Form a tech support team or identify tech ambassadors who can provide ongoing support to team members needing help with technology.

6. Interactive Tech Webinars

   Objective: To facilitate remote learning of technologies.

Activity: Host webinars where employees can learn about and ask questions regarding various tech tools and best practices.

7. Customized E-Learning Paths

Objective: To provide self-paced learning opportunities.

Activity: Create or use existing e-learning platforms to offer customized learning paths, allowing team members to learn about technologies at their own pace.

8. Discussion Forums

Objective: To allow employees to ask questions and share tech knowledge.

Activity: Create online forums or use existing platforms where team members can ask tech-related questions, share advice, or discuss new tools.

9. Role-Based Tech Training

Objective: To provide technology training relevant to each role.

Activity: Organize technology training sessions that are tailored to the specific roles and responsibilities of different team members, ensuring relevance.

10. Cross-Generational Project Teams

Objective: To promote practical application and collaboration.

Activity: Form project teams with mixed generations to allow members to learn from each other's tech expertise through practical collaboration and problem-solving.

Chapter 12:

Promoting Unity in Diversity: Strategies for a Collaborative and Inclusive Workplace

Creating an inclusive and collaborative work environment is critical to harness the diverse talents of a multigenerational team. This chapter provides practical strategies to foster unity in diversity and promote effective collaboration among all generations.

12.1 Inclusivity: The Key to Unity in Diversity

Inclusivity plays a pivotal role in leveraging the strengths of a diverse workforce. It goes beyond mere tolerance or acceptance; the goal is valuing and using the unique contributions that individuals from each generation bring to the table.

The Role of Belonging:

Inclusivity fosters a sense of belonging among employees, crucial for boosting engagement and productivity. According to a 2023

LinkedIn survey, feeling valued and having a sense of belonging at work were pivotal factors influencing job satisfaction across generations (Deutser, 2023). Another 2021 report by BetterUp showed that employees with a sense of belonging are 3.5 times more likely to be productive and engaged (Perry, 2021).

Proactive Inclusivity Efforts:

Achieving inclusivity necessitates deliberate actions and strategies beyond good intentions. For instance, a 2014 Catalyst study emphasized the need for fair policies, diverse leadership representation, and consistent diversity training (Prime & Salib, 2014). Companies like Apple exemplify proactivity in fostering inclusivity, revealed through their regular diversity reports and various inclusivity-focused initiatives.

Inclusivity is not merely a concept but an actionable strategy that, when properly implemented, leads to a more united, productive, and successful multigenerational workforce.

12.2 Building Bridges: Improving Collaboration Among Generations

Collaboration is a cornerstone in a multigenerational workforce, and it relies on clear and open communication. This ensures that ideas are shared effectively and that every team member, regardless of age, feels heard and valued. Effective communication acts as the glue that binds diverse perspectives, fostering an environment where innovation and collective problem-solving can flourish. It's the key to unlocking the full potential of a team's varied experiences and skills.

Leveraging Unique Strengths:

Recognizing and valuing the distinct skills of each generation is vital. Appreciating and using the unique abilities of each age group boosts collaboration. For example, General Electric encourages knowledge sharing across generations through programs such as reverse mentoring. As previously discussed, this involves pairing younger employees with senior team members, fostering an exchange of ideas and learnings.

Promoting Respect and Understanding:

Cultivating a work environment grounded in mutual respect and understanding is key to minimizing generational conflicts and bolstering collaboration. A report from the University of North Carolina in 2021 stresses the role of respect and understanding in enhancing cooperation among multigenerational teams (UNC, 2021). Companies like Adobe exemplify this approach. Adobe's Generation Adobe Network, for instance, assembles employees across generations to exchange experiences and ideas, promoting a culture of respect and mutual understanding.

Facilitating a collaborative environment where each generation feels valued enhances overall productivity and workplace harmony.

12.3 Overcoming Obstacles: Addressing Common Challenges in a Multigenerational Workplace

Addressing the common challenges that arise in a multigenerational workplace is essential for maintaining a harmonious and effective work environment.

Tackling Biases and Stereotypes:

Addressing biases and stereotypes is central to promoting inclusivity and collaboration. Generational stereotypes could significantly obstruct teamwork and productivity. IBM is a company that has made strides to tackle age biases, introducing initiatives like the Age Diversity Employee Resource Group to promote understanding and challenge age-related stereotypes.

Using Diversity Training:

Implementing diversity training is a powerful tool to nurture an understanding of generational variances. The Society for Human Resource Management, in a 2020 report, advocated for diversity training as a robust tactic to curtail generational conflicts and enhance understanding (Gurchiek, 2020). Companies like Mastercard have launched diversity training initiatives, which serve as platforms for employees to share experiences, learn, and cultivate mutual respect.

Promoting Feedback and Open Discussions:

Encouraging an environment where feedback and open discussions are the norm can be transformative in addressing workplace challenges. A 2022 article by Appelbaum et al, (2022) underscored the significance of feedback in resolving generational conflicts and bolstering collaboration. For example, at Google, they integrate a culture of feedback and encourage employees across generations to engage in open communication, fostering mutual understanding.

Specific activities, exercises, and strategies can help in building a collaborative and inclusive team. Each activity has a different focus to cater to various aspects of inclusivity and collaboration. Using a combination of these activities and leadership strategies can enhance the collaborative and inclusive nature of a team, making the workplace more harmonious and productive.

Activities & Exercises

1. "Walk in My Shoes" Exercise:

    Objective: To develop empathy and understanding among team members.

    Activity: Have team members pair up and share experiences or challenges they face in the workplace because of generational differences and discuss potential solutions or coping strategies.

2. Team-Building Workshops:

    Objective: To improve interpersonal relationships and communication.

    Activity: Conduct workshops that focus on team-building exercises, problem-solving tasks, and communication enhancement activities.

3. Round-Table Discussions:

    Objective: To facilitate open communication and idea sharing.

Activity: Organize sessions where each member can share their ideas or provide feedback openly. Ensure that everyone's voice is heard.

4. Cross-Generational Mentoring:

    Objective: To promote mutual learning and understanding.

    Activity: Pair up individuals from different generations for mutual mentoring sessions where they can learn from each other's experiences and perspectives.

5. Diversity and Inclusion Training:

    Objective: To educate team members about the importance of diversity and inclusion.

    Activity: Organize training sessions that focus on the value of diversity and provide tools and strategies for fostering an inclusive environment.

Leadership Strategies

1. Continuous Learning:

    Leaders should prioritize their own continuous learning to understand the dynamics of a multigenerational workforce better and to lead effectively.

2. Promote a Culture of Respect:

    Leaders should emphasize the importance of mutual respect, appreciation for diverse perspectives, and encourage a culture where everyone feels valued.

3. Open Door Policy:

    Leaders should maintain an open-door policy,

encouraging team members to communicate their ideas, feedback, or concerns freely.

4. Recognition and Appreciation:

Leaders should build a feeling of value and belonging in employees by acknowledging accomplishments.

5. Flexible Leadership Style:

Leaders should be adaptable in their leadership styles to cater to the diverse needs and preferences of a multigenerational team.

6. Encouraging Collaboration:

Leaders should encourage collaboration and promote unity and shared purpose.

7. Facilitating Learning Opportunities:

Leaders should facilitate learning opportunities, like workshops or seminars, that focus on enhancing collaboration and inclusivity skills among team members.

Chapter 13:

Strategies for Success

Multigenerational teams have become a common fixture. Individuals from diverse age groups compose these teams, each bringing their unique perspectives, experiences, and skills to the table. Multigenerational collaboration in the workplace marks an important change in how organizations operate and their cultures. When people from different generations work together, they bring a variety of ideas and perspectives to the table. This variety boosts creativity, improves problem-solving, and contributes to the success of the organization. Multigenerational teams symbolize diversity and inclusiveness in today's complicated work environment. These teams allow organizations to benefit from a wide range of talents and skills, improving their ability to adapt and stay competitive in a constantly changing business world.

The objective is to characterize multigenerational teams, laying a foundation for understanding and leveraging the manifold contributions that generational diversity brings to organizational life. Through a journey of exploration and discovery, this chapter provides strategies, insights, and outlines practical wisdom to manage the multifaceted world of multigenerational collaboration effectively.

13.1 Embracing Diversity in Multigenerational Teams

In multigenerational teams, diversity is a tremendous asset. Each generation brings its unique strengths, perspectives, and skills, contributing to a rich and dynamic team environment. Recognizing and valuing these unique contributions is essential for fostering a thriving team atmosphere.

First, it's vital to appreciate the distinctive qualities that each generation brings to the team. Baby Boomers often bring a wealth of experience and industry knowledge, while Generation X members offer a balance of traditional and modern insights, being adaptable and self-sufficient. Millennials are tech-savvy, valuing collaboration and innovation, and technological intuitiveness and global awareness characterizes Generation Z.

Creating an inclusive environment where all team members feel valued is fundamental. Such an environment encourages open communication, mutual respect, and the sharing of diverse ideas and viewpoints, driving team collaboration and innovation. Embracing generational diversity involves promoting a culture that appreciates the contributions of each individual and utilizes their unique strengths for team success. This involves cultivating a workspace that not only tolerates but celebrates differences, encouraging each member to bring their authentic selves to the team, thus bolstering productivity and job satisfaction.

In embracing diversity within multigenerational teams, organizations pave the way for enhanced creativity, problem-solving, and decision-making, setting the stage for sustained success and innovation in an ever-changing business landscape.

13.2 Crafting Effective Communication Strategies

Effective communication acts as the glue holding multigenerational teams together. It's crucial to adapt communication styles and tools to meet the diverse preferences present in a multigenerational team.

Different generations often have varied communication preferences, ranging from face-to-face interactions preferred by older generations to the inclination towards digital communication platforms by the younger generations. Understanding and respecting these preferences is essential to ensure that every team member feels heard and valued.

To enhance connectivity and understanding within the team, employing a mix of communication tools and platforms is beneficial. Supplement traditional methods, such as in-person meetings, phone calls, and emails, with modern tools like instant messaging, video conferencing, and collaboration platforms. This blended approach ensures that information is conveyed effectively and promptly, catering to the comfort and preferences of all team members.

In crafting communication strategies, the goal should always be clarity, conciseness, and inclusivity. Messages should be clear to prevent misunderstandings, and various communication channels should ensure information reaches all team members. Fostering an environment where open communication is encouraged and feedback is welcomed enhances team collaboration and problem-solving.

Ultimately, crafting effective communication strategies that cater to the diverse needs of a multigenerational team promotes a harmonious and productive work environment where every team member can thrive.

13.3 Cultivating a Collaborative Team Culture

Building a collaborative team culture where members are encouraged to share knowledge and leverage each other's strengths is essential for multigenerational teams. A conducive environment that values each member's input promotes intergenerational collaboration and leads to innovative problem-solving.

Strategies for Promoting Intergenerational Collaboration and Knowledge Sharing:

Encourage Open Dialogue: Promote an atmosphere where team members feel comfortable sharing their ideas and opinions, irrespective of their generational classification. Open dialogue fosters a sense of belonging and mutual respect among team members.

Facilitate Mentorship Programs: Implement mentorship programs where the experienced can share their knowledge, and the less experienced can offer fresh perspectives. This reciprocity enhances learning and professional development across all generations.

Techniques for Leveraging Diverse Skills and Perspectives for Innovative Problem-solving:

Diverse Team Projects: Create project teams with a mix of generational talents. The different skills and perspectives brought by each generation can offer various approaches to problem-solving, encouraging innovation.

Foster a culture of continuous learning where team members encourage each other to learn from one another. Webinars, workshops, and training sessions, where team members share knowledge, can be beneficial.

Celebrating Successes: Recognize and celebrate the team's successes, ensuring that the contributions of all generations are valued and appreciated. Recognition promotes motivation and a sense of accomplishment among team members.

Cultivating a collaborative team culture that leverages the diversity of multigenerational teams is crucial for innovation and success in the modern workplace. It not only enhances productivity but also contributes to the personal and professional growth of each team member.

13.4 Flexibility in Work Arrangements and Processes

Flexibility in the workplace is a key component that can enhance the productivity and satisfaction of multigenerational teams. Each generation comes with unique work styles and preferences, and a flexible approach helps to accommodate these diverse needs.

Importance of Flexibility in Accommodating Different Work Styles and Preferences:

Adaptability: A flexible work environment is adaptable. It allows modifications according to the diverse needs and preferences of each team member, ensuring that everyone can perform at their best.

Customization: Flexibility enables the customization of work arrangements. Different generations have varied work habits and preferences, and a one-size-fits-all approach might not be effective. Customized work arrangements ensure that the needs of all generations are met.

Implementing Flexible Work Policies that Support Productivity and Work-life Balance:

Remote Work and Flexible Hours: Offering options, such as remote work and flexible hours, can be beneficial. Such policies allow team members to choose work arrangements that best suit their lifestyles, promoting a healthy work-life balance.

Clear Guidelines: While promoting flexibility, it's also essential to have clear guidelines. Policies should be clear on expectations, communication, and deadlines.

Continuous evaluation of flexible work policies is necessary to ensure that they meet the team's current needs. Feedback from team members can help to make necessary adjustments.

By implementing flexibility in work arrangements and processes, organizations can create a supportive environment where each generation feels valued and motivated, enhancing overall productivity and team satisfaction.

13.5 Promoting Continuous Learning and Development

Continuous learning and development are crucial in multigenerational teams for keeping skills updated and promoting adaptability to changing work environments. Encouraging a culture of lifelong learning can help enhance the team's overall capabilities and accommodate the diverse learning needs of each generation.

Encouraging Lifelong Learning for Enhanced Skills and Adaptability:

Cultivating a Growth Mindset: Encourage team members to embrace a growth mindset where they are open to learning and improving continually. This mindset fosters adaptability and a willingness to evolve with changing industry trends and technologies.

Providing Opportunities for Skill Development: Organizations should provide various opportunities for team members to develop and enhance their skills continually. This could include workshops, webinars, or courses that are available to all team members.

Using Various Learning Platforms and Resources to Cater to Diverse Learning Needs:

Leveraging Online Platforms: Online learning platforms offer a range of resources catering to different learning styles and needs. They can be effective in reaching multigenerational team members, each with their own learning preferences.

Offering Varied Learning Resources: Providing a mix of learning resources such as articles, videos, and interactive modules can cater to different learning preferences, ensuring that all team members have access to resources that suit their learning style.

Customizing Learning Paths: Consider the unique learning needs of each generation and customize learning paths accordingly. This might mean offering more hands-on training for some or providing self-paced online modules for others.

Promoting continuous learning and development is essential to ensure that multigenerational teams remain adaptable, skilled, and prepared to meet the evolving demands of the workplace.

13.6 Mentorship and Knowledge Sharing: Bridging the Generational Gap

Mentorship and knowledge sharing are powerful tools for bridging the generational gap in multigenerational teams. They foster an environment where team members can learn from each other's experiences, insights, and knowledge, promoting reciprocal learning and mutual respect.

Implementing Mutual Mentorship Programs for Reciprocal Learning:

Developing Mentorship Programs: Establish mentorship programs that allow for mutual mentorship, where team members from different generations can learn from each other. This could involve a younger team member mentoring an older team member in areas such as technology, while the older team member mentors on industry experience and professional guidance.

Promoting Reciprocal Learning: Ensure that the mentorship programs promote a two-way street of learning where both parties benefit from the exchange. This encourages participation and engagement in the mentorship process.

Facilitating Platforms for Knowledge Exchange and Shared Experience:

Creating Opportunities for Discussion: Encourage sharing experiences and knowledge. Regular team meetings, discussion forums, or informal gatherings could be implemented.

Leveraging Technology: use technology to facilitate knowledge sharing, such as creating online platforms or forums where team members can share insights, ask questions, and engage in discussions.

Encouraging Openness: Promote an open environment where team members feel comfortable sharing their thoughts and experiences without judgment. This fosters a supportive environment, ensuring teams feel valued and heard.

Implementing mentorship and knowledge sharing initiatives are vital strategies in making the most of the diverse strengths, experiences, and knowledge present within multigenerational teams, ultimately contributing to the team's success and cohesion.

13.7 Leadership in Multigenerational Teams

Leadership plays a pivotal role in guiding multigenerational teams towards success. The leader helps to promote a culture of inclusivity, mutual respect, and harmonious collaboration among team members of various age groups. Here are the focal areas where leadership can make a significant impact:

Role of Leaders in Promoting Inclusivity and Mutual Respect:

Fostering Inclusivity: Leaders should cultivate a workspace where every team member, regardless of their generational classification, feels included and valued. They should encourage participation and give equal opportunities for every team member to voice their opinions and ideas.

Encouraging Mutual Respect: Leaders must set the tone for mutual respect within the team. By showing appreciation for the diverse skills and perspectives that each generation brings, leaders can encourage team members to value each other's contributions and experiences.

Developing Leadership Strategies that Support Diverse Team Dynamics:

Adaptable Leadership Styles: Leaders should be adaptable in their leadership styles to cater to the varied preferences and motivations of different generations. Understanding what drives each team member and tailoring leadership strategies to meet their needs is essential.

Communication: Effective communication strategies should ensure clear and concise information flow. Leaders should also be open to feedback and create channels through which team members can express their thoughts and concerns freely.

Support and guidance: Leaders should offer consistent support and guidance to team members, facilitating their professional growth and development. It entails recognizing the distinct requirements and capabilities of every team member and offering the necessary resources.

13.8 Challenges in Multigenerational Teams

Multigenerational teams, despite their many benefits, come with their own set of challenges. It's imperative to identify these obstacles early and implement proactive strategies to navigate through them effectively. Here are some common issues and how they can be mitigated:

Identifying Common Obstacles:

Stereotypes: Preconceived notions or stereotypes about different generations can hinder collaboration. For instance, people might see older employees as resistant to change, while they may view younger ones as lacking professionalism or experience.

Communication Barriers: Varied communication preferences across generations can lead to misunderstandings or information gaps. Older generations might prefer formal communication channels, while younger ones may favor instant messaging or social media platforms.

Implementing Proactive Strategies:

Challenge Stereotypes: Promote a culture that challenges stereotypes and encourages team members to appreciate each other's strengths. Open discussions about generational differences, workshops, and team-building activities can be useful strategies.

Encouraging Open Communication: Foster a communication-friendly environment where team members feel comfortable sharing their thoughts, opinions, and feedback. Clarify that every voice is valued and ensure that various communication platforms cater to everyone's preferences.

Adaptability: Encourage adaptability and openness to different approaches and perspectives. This can involve promoting a learning mindset where team members are open to gaining new skills and adapting to varied communication styles or work processes.

By recognizing and addressing these challenges proactively, multigenerational teams can function more harmoniously and efficiently, leveraging the diverse strengths that each generation brings to the table.

13.9 Case Studies: Best Practices in Managing Multigenerational Teams

In this section, we delve into real-life case studies that showcase the successful management and collaboration of multigenerational teams. These examples provide practical insights into how various organizations have fostered environments where diversity in age is a strength rather than a hindrance. Let's uncover the key takeaways and lessons from these organizational experiences.

Case Study 1: A technology company leveraged its multigenerational workforce to innovate its product offerings. Younger employees brought fresh perspectives and technological savviness, while older team members contributed industry wisdom and extensive experience. By promoting cross-generational mentorship and collaboration, the company could develop groundbreaking products that were well-received in the market.

Key Takeaways:

Mutual mentorship can foster a reciprocal learning environment.

Collaboration between generations can fuel innovation and product development.

Case Study 2: A healthcare organization implemented flexible work arrangements to cater to its diverse workforce. This approach respected the different life stages and priorities of its employees, ranging from new parents to those nearing retirement. As a result, employee satisfaction and retention rates improved significantly.

Key Takeaways:

Flexible work policies can meet the diverse needs of a multigenerational workforce.

Consideration of employees' life stages enhances job satisfaction and loyalty.

Case Study 3: An enterprise introduced various communication platforms to cater to its multigenerational team members. Traditional email communications coexisted with modern collaboration tools like instant messaging and project management apps. This strategy enhanced connectivity and streamlined workflows across the team.

Key Takeaways:

Diverse communication tools can bridge the gap between different generational preferences.

Adaptability in communication strategies can improve overall team collaboration and efficiency.

These case studies illuminate the potential of multigenerational teams to drive organizational success. The lessons learned underscore the importance of adaptability, inclusivity, and continual learning to manage diverse teams effectively.

Conclusion

Harnessing the multigenerational workforce has shown the intricate dynamics of the modern, diverse workplace, unveiling the unique characteristics, values, and work styles of Baby Boomers, Gen X, Millennials, and Gen Z, and their profound impact on organizational culture and productivity.

Throughout these pages, we have outlined the formidable power and inherent challenges of managing a multigenerational workforce, showcasing the vibrant potential for unprecedented innovation, coupled with the risks of conflicts and misunderstandings. We examined the generational communication styles, the construction of trustful professional relationships, and the manifestation of adaptive leadership suited to guide a multigenerational battalion of talents.

We have placed an emphasis on the necessity to dispel generational biases and stereotypes and champion the embrace of technological metamorphoses to cultivate an atmosphere of inclusivity, respect, and collaboration.

Key Takeaways:

Respect and Understanding: Fundamental in transforming generational diversity into a wellspring of innovation and productivity.

Adaptive Leadership: A beacon that guides the confluence of generational strengths, fostering an environment ripe for innovation and organizational growth.

Overcoming Challenges: Strategic addressing of biases, stereotypes, and the technological hesitance of older workers unfolds an inclusive, collaborative, and productive workplace canvas.

Embracing generational diversity is more than just a necessity—it's a significant catalyst for organizational success. The fusion of unique perspectives, experiences, and skills across different age groups enriches the team, driving innovation, adaptability, and a robust problem-solving capacity. Organizations that successfully manage and integrate these generational differences are better positioned to navigate the complexities of the modern business environment, showcasing resilience, creativity, and a strong sense of unity in pursuit of common objectives. Thus, in the synthesis of varied generational contributions, organizations find a profound and enriching pathway to thrive and excel in their respective industries.

Share Your Journey:

Thank you for investing your time in reading our book! Your thoughts and feedback are invaluable to us and other readers. We invite you to share your insights, experiences, and the impact this book has had on your perspective of multigenerational teams by writing a review. Your unique viewpoint will not only enhance the learning of others, but also contribute significantly to our journey of continuous improvement and development. We are eager to hear from you and appreciate your willingness to engage with us and the broader reader community! Thank you for your support!

References

ABDO. (2018). *Reverse mentoring: A win-win for mentor & mentee.* ABDO Business Support Hub. https://www.abdo.org.uk/wp-content/uploads/2018/04/ABDO-BSH-Reverse-mentoring-A-win-win-for-mentor-and-mentee-i.pdf

Accenture. (2024). Student Leadership Program. https://www.accenture.com/us-en/careers/local/accenture-student-leadership-program.

Aggarwal, N., Cowls, J. Floridi, L., Mokander, J., Morley, J., Taddeo, M., Tsamados, A., Wang, V., & Watson, D. (2020, July 7). *Covid-19 and the digital divides.* Oxford Internet Institute. https://www.oii.ox.ac.uk/news-events/news/covid-19-and-the-digital-divides/

Answernet Admin. (2024, February 13). *How each generation communicates.* Answernet. https://answernet.com/blog-generations-styles-communication

Appelbaum, S. H., Bhardwaj, A., Goodyear, M., Gong, T., Sudha, A. B., & Wei, P. (2022). A Study of Generational Conflicts in the Workplace. European Journal of Business andManagementResearch7.https://www.researchgate.net/publication/359246915_A_Study_of_Generational_Conflicts_in_the_Workplace

Bourke, J. (2016, April 14). *The six signature traits of inclusive leadership.* Deloitte Insights.

https://www2.deloitte.com/us/en/insights/topics/tale
nt/six-signature-traits-of-inclusive-leadership.html

Bourke, J. & Dillon, B. (2018, January). The diversity and inclusion revolution. *Deloitte Review, 22.*
https://www2.deloitte.com/content/dam/insights/us/
articles/4209_Diversity-and-inclusion-
revolution/DI_Diversity-and-inclusion-revolution.pdf

Brady, B. (2019, September 5). *The power of reverse mentoring.* Forbes.
https://www.forbes.com/sites/forbesagencycouncil/2
019/09/05/the-power-of-reverse-mentoring/

Brown, J. (2019). *How to be an inclusive leader: Creating trust, cooperation, and community across differences.* Berrett-Koehler.
https://www.amazon.com.au/How-Inclusive-Leader-
Cooperation-Differences/dp/1523085177

Brown, S., & Robison, J. (2020, May 21). *How to communicate to create stability despite uncertainty.* Gallup Workplace.
https://www.gallup.com/workplace/311288/communi
cate-create-stability-despite-uncertainty.aspx

Burnison, G. (2019, February 28). *7 years ago, Google set out to find what makes the 'perfect' team—and what they found shocked other researchers.* CNBC.
https://www.cnbc.com/2019/02/28/what-google-
learned-in-its-quest-to-build-the-perfect-team.html

Clark, S, (2022, May 3). *Generational differences and how they affect workplace dynamics.* Reworked.
https://www.reworked.co/talent-
management/generational-differences-and-how-they-
affect-workplace-dynamics/

Cloverpop. (2018). *Hacking diversity with inclusive decision-making.* https://www.cloverpop.com/hacking-diversity-with-inclusive-decision-making-white-paper

Deloitte. (2023). 2023 *Gen Z and Millennial survey.* https://www.deloitte.com/global/en/issues/work/content/genzmillennialsurvey.html

DePaul, K, & Sawhney, V. (2022, March 8). *Is generational prejudice seeping into your workplace?* Harvard Business Review. https://hbr.org/2022/03/is-generational-prejudice-seeping-into-your-workplace

DePrisco, M. (2011, February 11). *Effective collaboration requires more than just communication.* Forbes. https://www.forbes.com/sites/forbesbusinesscouncil/2022/02/11/effective-collaboration-requires-more-than-just-communication/?sh=756059165fe6

Deutser, B. (2023, September 20). *Our research on the power of belonging in the workplace.* LinkedIn. https://www.linkedin.com/pulse/our-research-power-belonging-workplace-brad-deutser

Ernst & Young LLP. (2023, December 6). The artificial intelligence (AI) boom across all industries has fueled anxiety in the workforce. PRNewswire.

Ely, R. J., & Thomas, D. A. (2020). Getting serious about diversity: Enough already with the business case. Harvard Business Review. https://hbr.org/2020/11/getting-serious-about-diversity-enough-already-with-the-business-case

Francis, T., & Hoefel, F. (2018, November). *'True Gen': Generation Z and its implications for companies.* McKinsey. https://www.mckinsey.com/~/media/mckinsey/indus

tries/consumer%20packaged%20goods/our%20insight
s/true%20gen%20generation%20z%20and%20its%20i
mplications%20for%20companies/generation-z-and-
its-implication-for-companies.pdf

Frei, F., & Moriss, A. (2020, June). *Begin with trust*. Harvard
Business Review. https://hbr.org/2020/05/begin-with-
trust

Fry, R. (2018, April 11). *Millennials are the largest generation in the
U.S. labor force*. Pew Research Center.
https://www.pewresearch.org/short-
reads/2018/04/11/millennials-largest-generation-us-
labor-force/

Fry, R. (2019, July 24). *Baby Boomers are staying in the labor force at
rates not seen in generations for people their age*. Pew Research
Center.   https://www.pewresearch.org/short-
reads/2019/07/24/baby-boomers-us-labor-force

Gartner Research. (2019, December 11). *Assessing the impact of
Microsoft Teams becoming as common as Outlook*.
https://www.gartner.com/en/documents/3976203

Garvin, D., Berkeley Wagonfeld, A., & Kind, L. (2013, April).
Google's Project Oxygen: Do managers matter? Harvard
Business   School.
https://www.hbs.edu/faculty/Pages/item.aspx?num=4
4657

Georges, L. (2019, April 24). *How generational stereotypes hold us back
at   work*.   TedX.
https://www.ted.com/talks/leah_georges_how_genera
tional_stereotypes_hold_us_back_at_work?language=e
n

Green, A. P., Eigel, L. M., James, J. B., Hartmann, D., & McLean, K. C. (2012). *Multiple generations in the workplace: Exploring the research, influence of stereotypes, and organizational applications.* In The Oxford Handbook of Work and Aging (pp. 484–500). https://academic.oup.com/edited-volume/28315/chapter/215052789

Gurchiek, K. (2020, October 22). *7 best practices to confront age bias, build generational diversity.* SHRM. https://www.shrm.org/resourcesandtools/hr-topics/behavioral-competencies/global-and-cultural-effectiveness/pages/7-best-practices-to-confront-age-bias-build-generational-diversity--.aspx

Hennelly, D., Schurman, B. (2023, January 5). Bridging Generational Divides in Your Workplace. Harvard Business Review. https://hbr.org/2023/01/bridging-generational-divides-in-your-workplace

Hunt, V., Yee, L., & Dixon-Fyle, S. (2018, January 18). *Delivering through diversity.* McKinsey. https://www.mckinsey.com/business-functions/organization/our-insights/delivering-through-diversity

IBM. (2020). *IBM 2020 diversity & inclusion report.* https://www.ibm.com/impact/be-equal/pdf/IBM_Diversity_Inclusion_Report_2020.pdf

Jackson, A. (n.d.). *Everyone can use a little bit of oxygen.* LifeAtATTBlog. https://life.att.jobs/article-oxygen-heather/

Jiang, Z. (2019, November 14). *Why withholding information at work won't give you an advantage.* Harvard Business Review.

https://hbr.org/2019/11/why-withholding-information-at-work-wont-give-you-an-advantage

Johnson & Johnson. (2023). *Generation Now.* https://www.jnj.com/diversity/employee-resource-groups/generation-now

Jordan, J., & Sorell, M. (2019). Why Reverse Mentoring Works and How to Do It Right. Harvard Business Review. https://hbr.org/2019/10/why-reverse-mentoring-works-and-how-to-do-it-right

Livingston, G. (2019, June 18). *Americans 60 and older are spending more time in front of their screens than a decade ago.* Pew Research Center. https://www.pewresearch.org/short-reads/2019/06/18/americans-60-and-older-are-spending-more-time-in-front-of-their-screens-than-a-decade-ago/

Livingston, R. (2021). *The conversation: How seeking and speaking the truth about racism can radically transform individuals and organizations.* Currency. https://robertwlivingston.com/books/the-conversation/

Mathuros, F. (2019, January 25). *World Economic Forum annual meeting 2019 closes with initiatives to address global problems.* World Economic Forum. https://www.weforum.org/press/2019/01/world-economic-annual-meeting-2019-closes-with-initiatives-to-address-global-problems

Microsoft 365 Team. (2019). *Collaboration, communication key to successful multi-generational, multi-cultural workplaces.* Microsoft. https://www.microsoft.com/en-us/microsoft-365/business-insights-ideas/resources/key-to-successful-multi-generational-workplaces

Murrell, A. (2017). *Mentoring diverse leaders: Creating change for people, processes, and paradigms.* Routledge. https://www.amazon.com.au/Mentoring-Diverse-Leaders-Processes-Paradigms/dp/1138814334

Nkomo, S.M. (1996). Diverse indentities in organizations. Sage Publications. https://scholar.google.com/citations?view_op=view_citation&hl=en&user=Ix6v9kEAAAAJ&citation_for_view=Ix6v9kEAAAAJ:u-x6o8ySG0sC

O'Flaherty, S., Sanders, M., & Whillans, A. (2021, March 29). *Research: A little recognition can provide a big morale boost.* https://hbr.org/2021/03/research-a-little-recognition-can-provide-a-big-morale-boost

Otiji-Spizler, A. (2019). *Cross-generational collaboration in the workplace* [Doctoral thesis, Northeastern University]. https://repository.library.northeastern.edu/files/neu:m044wx34g/fulltext.pdf

Parker, K., & Igielnik, R. (2020, May 14). On the cusp of adulthood and facing an uncertain future: What we know about Gen Z so far. Pew Research Center.

Pasternak, B. (2024). From teenage app developer to tech entrepreneur: The Ben Pasternak journey. Journal of Business and Technology, 11(2), 34-56.

Pandey, E. (2022, February 25). *The Great Resignation generation: Gen Z wants to job hop.* Axios Finish Line. https://www.axios.com/2022/02/25/gen-z-great-resignation-generation-job-hopping

Pendell, R., & Vander Helm, S. (2022, November 11). *Generation disconnected: Data on Gen Z in the workplace*. Gallup. https://www.gallup.com/workplace/404693/generatio n-disconnected-data-gen-workplace.aspx

Perry, E. (2021, May 11). *Here's how to build a sense of belonging in the workplace*. BetterUp. https://www.betterup.com/blog/belonging

Pollak, L. (2019). *The remix: How to lead and succeed in the multigenerational workplace*. HarperCollins. https://www.amazon.com.au/Remix-Lead-Succeed-Multigenerational-Workplace/dp/0062880217

Polman, P. (2013, October 2). Interview: Unilever's Paul Polman on diversity, purpose and profits. The Guardian.

Prime, J. & Salib, E. (2014). *Inclusive leadership: The view from six countries*. Catalyst. https://www.catalyst.org/research/inclusive-leadership-the-view-from-six-countries/

Public Affairs. (2017). *Change at work linked to employee stress, distrust, and intent to quit, new survey finds*. American Psychological Association. https://www.apa.org/news/press/releases/2017/05/e mployee-stress

PwC. (2021). Diversity, equity and inclusion consulting. https://www.pwc.com/us/en/services/consulting/bus iness-transformation/workforce-transformation/diversity-inclusion-consulting.html

Ramalingam, B., Nabarro, D., Oqubay, A., Carnall, R., & Wild, L. (2020, September 11). *5 principles to guide adaptive leadership*. Harvard Business Review.

https://hbr.org/2020/09/5-principles-to-guide-adaptive-leadership

Relihan, T. (2018, May 11). How Costco's obsession with culture drove success. MIT Management Sloan School. https://mitsloan.mit.edu/ideas-made-to-matter/how-costcos-obsession-culture-drove-success

Reynolds, A., & Lewis, D. (2018). The Two Traits of the Best Problem-Solving Teams. Harvard Business Review. https://hbr.org/2018/04/the-two-traits-of-the-best-problem-solving-teams

Rock, D., & Grant, H. (2016). Why diverse teams are smarter. Harvard Business Review. Rock, D., & Grant, H. (2016). Why diverse teams are smarter. Harvard Business Review.

Sabatini Henelly, D., & Schurman, B. (2023, January 5). *Bridging generational divides in your workplace.* Harvard Business Review. https://hbr.org/2023/01/bridging-generational-divides-in-your-workplace

Schaubroeck, R., Holsztejn, F., & Theunissen, R. (2016, March 3). *Making collaboration across functions a reality.* McKinsey & Company https://www.mckinsey.com/capabilities/people-and-organizational-performance/our-insights/making-collaboration-across-functions-a-reality

Sharma, S. (2019, June 4). *Hybrid integration platforms: Digital business calls for integration modernization and greater agility.* IBM. https://www.ibm.com/downloads/cas/EQZMDZAG

Snyder, B. (2004, April 1). *Deborah Gruenfeld: Diverse teams produce better decisions.* Stanford Graduate School of Business.

https://www.gsb.stanford.edu/insights/deborah-gruenfeld-diverse-teams-produce-better-decisions

Stanford Business. (n.d.). *Leadership*. https://www.gsb.stanford.edu/experience/learning/leadership

Stanford GSB Staff. (1999, November 1). *Diversity and work group performance*. Stanford Business. https://www.gsb.stanford.edu/insights/diversity-work-group-performance

Swanson, J. A., Renes, S. L., & Strange, A. T. (2018). The communication preferences of collegiate students. 15th International Conference on Cognition and Exploratory Learning in Digital Age (CELDA 2018) (pp. 86-93).

Together. (n.d.). *Successful mentoring programs to inspire your own.* https://www.togetherplatform.com/blog/examples-of-successful-mentoring-programs

UNC. (2021). A *guide to leading the multigenerational workforce.* University of North Carolina. https://onlinemba.unc.edu/wp-content/uploads/sites/10/2021/05/Final_Multigenerational_Workforce_Guide_Optimized_Trial.pdf

Velumyan, N. (2019, September 4). How to develop effective communication within a company. Forbes.

Venter, E. (2017). Bridging the communication gap between Generation Y and the Baby Boomer generation. *International Journal of Adolescence and Youth, 22:4*, 497–507, DOI: 10.1080/02673843.2016.1267022

Waldstreicher, J. (2021, June 10). *How Johnson & Johnson made hard decisions during covid.* Harvard Business Review.

https://hbr.org/2021/06/how-johnson-johnson-made-hard-decisions-during-covid

Walmart. (2021). *Belonging begins with us: 2021 CDEI Report.* https://corporate.walmart.com/content/dam/corporate/documents/purpose/culture-diversity-equity-and-inclusion-report/2021-cdei-annual-report.pdf

Wiest, B. (2019, November 4). *Millennials hate phone calls, and they have a point.* Forbes. https://www.forbes.com/sites/briannawiest/2019/11/04/millennials-hate-phone-calls-they-have-a-point

3M. (2020). Unlocking the Benefits of the Multigenerational Workplace. Harvard Business Review. https://www.harvardbusiness.org/wp-content/uploads/2020/08/Unlocking-the-Benefits-of-Multigenerational-Workforces_Aug-2020.pdf